Hospitality:
Life without Fear

*Finding Meaning and Purpose
In a Fearful World*

Steve Clapp and Fred Bernhard

Cover by Custom Maid Design

A LifeQuest Publication

Hospitality:
Life without Fear

Finding Meaning and Purpose
In a Fearful World

Steve Clapp and Fred Bernhard

For further information, contact: LifeQuest, 6404 S. Calhoun Street, Fort Wayne, Indiana 46807. 219-744-6510. DadofTia@aol.com

The authors of this book are not law enforcement professionals, home security experts, weather authorities, or Internet gurus. This book is not intended as a resource for safe living but as a guide to a spiritually based hospitality, which helps us live less fearfully.

Biblical quotations, unless otherwise noted, are from the New Revised Standard Version of the Bible, copyrighted 1989 by the Division of Christian Education, National Council of Churches, and are used by permission.

ISBN 1-893270-04-1

Manufactured in the United States of America

Contents

Rather than a traditional table of contents, we've chosen to include not only the chapter titles but also the core concept which is covered in each chapter.

This book is dedicated to:

The memory of my parents, who taught me by example the meaning of hospitality, and to my Christian Community colleagues, whose continuing hospitality enriches my life: Jan Fairchild, Kristen Leverton Helbert, Pat Helman, Jerry Peterson, Holly Sprunger, Sara Sprunger, and Angela Zizak.

Steve Clapp

And to:

Professor Don Miller and President Eugene Roop of Bethany Theological Seminary, whose encouragement led me to the exploration of this biblical teaching, and to the Oakland congregation, who walked the faith walk and made Christ's welcome incarnate.

Fred Bernhard

We both extend our thanks for the contributions made to this book by: Kristen Leverton Helbert, Celia King, Claire Long, Randy Maid, and the staff of Evangel Press.

So we have known and believe the love that God has for us. God is love, and those who abide in love abide in God, and God abides in them. Love has been perfected among us in this: that we may have boldness on the day of judgment, because as he is, so are we in this world. There is no fear in love, but perfect love casts out fear; for fear has to do with punishment; and whoever fears has not reached perfection in love.

We love because he first loved us. Those who say,"I love God," and hate their brothers or sisters, are liars; for those who do not love a brother or sister whom they have seen, cannot love God whom they have not seen.

1 John 4:16-20

Introduction
Why We Wrote This Book

Steve was washing his hands in the men's room at a restaurant when an eight-year-old boy in the room broke into tears. When Steve asked him what the problem was, the tearful response was: "My zipper's stuck in my underwear. I can't get my pants to zip. And I can't go out there like this. Can you help me?" Steve would have preferred being faced with almost any other dilemma! In some earlier generations, a decent man would have thought relatively little about giving help to a child with such a problem. In our time, that kind of help has the potential to lead to horrible misunderstanding and even legal consequences.

The eight-year-old adamantly refused to leave the men's room to get help from his mother, and his father was not at the restaurant. Steve found his mother in the hall, introduced himself, and explained her son's problem. She didn't want to go into the men's room, and her son still refused to come out. The mother asked Steve to fix the zipper, and it was easy for him to do so.

Fred was working in the late afternoon at his office after the rest of the church staff had gone home. He responded to a rap at the office door and discovered a very distraught, middle-aged woman who wanted to talk. She was an acquaintance from the community rather than a member of the church or a close friend. She wanted Fred to hear her story and offer advice on a major problem in her life.

In Fred's earlier ministry, that request would have been granted without question. In today's climate, that kind of request under those circumstances posed two potential dangers for Fred. First, it can be considered unwise for a man to be alone with a woman with no one else in the building. Second, she was seeking professional advice but Fred's credentials are as a minister rather than a psychologist or psychiatrist. Fred had three options for responding to her: he could refuse to see her; he could set an appointment to visit with her at a future time when others were in the building; or he could grant her request, setting some boundaries for her expectations of him and taking the risk.

We live in a wonderful age. At the time of the writing of this book, the economy in North America is strong, unemployment is low, and many people are enjoying a relatively high standard of living. Advances in medication and in medical procedures have increased the life expectancy and improved the quality of life for many people. Computer technology and the continued development of the Internet have greatly improved our access to information and the speed of our communication with others.

But we also live in a fearful time. No intelligent, sensitive man would give help to a boy like the one Steve encountered without parental permission. Both Steve and the mother had to come to a decision of mutual trust, on the basis of very little information about each other, before the boy's dilemma could be resolved. Her son didn't care about their anxieties; he simply wanted his zipper fixed. The woman who approached Fred for help dealing with her immediate pain was not aware of the dilemma which her presence posed for him. He responded to her positively but not without risk.

Many of us are not comfortable around strangers, and some of us aren't sure how far to trust our friends and work colleagues. Our time is often called the Information Age, and that is a reasonable description. Some of that information, however, has made us painfully aware of the worst of which human beings are capable. It is an Age of Fear as well as of information.

If It Bleeds, It Leads

"If it bleeds, it leads" is an old journalist guideline; but it has tremendous impact on radio, television, and Internet reporting as well as on newspapers and magazines. While the violent crime rate in the United States has decreased in recent years, reporting of crime continues to increase. According to one study by the Center for Media and Public Affairs, the television coverage of murder increased by 336% between 1995 and 2000.

Following the tragedy at Columbine High School in Littleton, Colorado, juvenile crime has come under very close scrutiny by the news media. Actions which would have received almost no publicity twenty years ago now become the subjects of headlines. Barry Glassner, a sociology professor and author of *The Culture of Fear*, says, "The images of young people running from Columbine have been shown hundreds of times. I don't mean to minimize the seriousness of the incident, but it gives the impression it's still with us, and that these kinds of events happen more often than they do" [Quoted in *The Desert Sun*, October 17, 1999]. News media reporting on both natural and human tragedy keeps some of us in perpetual fear of flying, driving, or sharing in social gatherings–including school. The news media, of course, are only part of the problem. Many play on our fears:

- Politicians want us to be afraid of crime and to have confidence that their "get tough" policies will keep us safe. Most of us, in our more rational moments, have learned not to believe everything we hear from politicians; but the emphasis they place on crime, as an election issue and as a continuing budget issue, affects all of us.

- Many television dramas and motion pictures feed our fears. We may find a certain measure of enjoyment in the charge of adrenalin that comes from fear during a show, but the memory of the fear often stays with us and affects our view of the world–even though we are not likely to face the evils that Mel Gibson, Sarah Michelle Gellar, Denzel Washington, and Sigourney Weaver do on the screen.

- Social service organizations sometimes appeal to our fears of drugs and violence in the process of raising money for their good work. Some of the best fund-raising appeals for organizations that work directly with children remind us of the dangers in our society.

- Ministers, including (we are embarrassed to confess) the authors of this book, talk about the dangers in our society as we call people to greater reliance on God. The call to lives more centered on God is an appropriate message for every age, but we some-times foster an "us" (in the church) versus "them" (in the world) way of looking at life.

- Some clergy and political groups have appealed to

the rampant fear of homosexuality in our society to build financial support and ballot box support for measures that fail to acknowledge the human rights of persons of homosexual orientation. The fear of homosexuality which has been engendered in some heterosexual people is both irrational and destructive.

• Real estate agents, builders, and security system companies may emphasize neighborhood crime rates, the possibility of burglary, and the need for home security as they sell houses and services. Some people now live in apartment buildings and housing complexes which give the appearance of being fortresses, designed to keep the occupants safe from danger.

And of course there are many other kinds of fear which affect us. We fear the illness or death of our loved ones; we fear our own illness or death; we fear financial catastrophe; we fear letting down the people who count on us; and we fear that we are not making the most of the opportunities God has given us.

Not all fears are bad or harmful. Fear of fires, tornadoes, hurricanes, and earthquakes helps people exercise caution which saves lives. Fear of illness motivates us to get medical care and to make lifestyle improvements. **Psalm 111:10** reminds us that: "The fear of the LORD is the beginning of wisdom; all those who practice it have a good understanding." The quote from First John opposite the first page of this Introduction maintains that "perfect love casts out fear." But most of us have not achieved that kind of love; and there are many of us who might do well to cultivate a healthy fear of God, particularly in terms of obedience.

A Different Way

Many of our fears, particularly those concerning strangers and our safety, have the ability to paralyze us from meaningful relationships. The truth is that many of us do not know how to relate comfortably to strangers; and we sometimes do not know how to relate comfortably to our spouses, children, parents, friends, and coworkers.

We are writing this book because we are convinced that there is a different way of living—one which closes the distance between ourselves and other people. That way of living is impossible unless our lives are rooted in God. We are convinced that God is calling all of us to lives of true biblical hospitality, that we need to increasingly view those around us as gifts from God and to recognize the presence of Christ in others, including those we may at first be tempted to dislike or even disown.

Henri Nouwen, in his classic book *Reaching Out*, said this about the world in which we live:

> *In our world full of strangers, estranged from their past, culture and country, from their neighbors, friends, and family, from their deepest self and their God, we witness a painful search for a hospitable place where life can be lived without fear and where community can be found* [p. 46].

Our lives do not have to be filled with fear. While there are dangerous elements in the world, the truth is that all of us were created out of the love of God; and creation is fundamentally good. For us, hospitality can be defined in this way:

> **Hospitality** involves recognizing the presence of Christ in family, friends, coworkers, neighbors, and complete strangers. It means responding to others as we would respond to the presence of Christ in our midst.

One of the major themes of this book is that blessings flow to us as we recognize the presence of Christ in others and reach out to one another. A life grounded in hospitality, a life which seeks to recognize the presence of Christ in each person we encounter, is not always going to be an easy life. It is often easier to be driven by our fears and to stay removed from others. But that kind of life is not the one to which God has called us.

Hospitality, of course, is not always safe. There's a small chance that someone we choose to befriend will turn out to be manipulative or dishonest. We may occasionally extend hospitality toward those who reject us. We may find that the practice of hospitality leads us into contact with persons we would otherwise have avoided. But the potential for blessings from a life centered in hospitality is much greater than the risks which are involved. If we take our relationships with God seriously, hospitality is not an optional way of living. When we fail to recognize the presence of Christ in others, we are in fact cutting ourselves off from the blessings God wishes to give us.

More Than You Wanted to Know About Us

We met each other in 1995 at an Evangelism Leaders Academy at Bridgewater College in Virginia. Both of us were giving leadership at that event; and we were introduced to each other by Paul Mundey, who was the director of The Andrew Center, which had sponsored the Academy.

Paul assumed correctly that we would enjoy visiting with each other, but he had more in mind. Steve had been conducting research on how effective congregations are at welcoming and accepting both visitors and members. Fred had initiated a major emphasis on hospitality in the congregation he pastored, and his church had experienced impressive growth as a result of that emphasis. Paul hoped the two of us would collaborate on a book, and we did just that. *Widening the Welcome of Your Church* was the result, and we continue to be pleased with the wonderful reception it has had around North America. The book has been reprinted four times with minor changes at each printing.

The two of us had been considering a major revision to the book, but we began to realize that many of the new concepts we wanted to develop were in fact related not to congregational life but to the spiritual lives of individuals–including those who have very little contact with the institutional church. While we will continue to refine *Widening the Welcome of Your Church* as reprints are made, we decided it was time to collaborate on a new book. You hold the result in your hands.

While some people will study and discuss this book as part of a church or community class or group, we have written this book primarily for individuals who are seeking to grow closer to God and to other people. Some who are reading these pages may not be active in any congregation and may in fact be so disillusioned with the institutional church that they can't conceive of ever belonging to one.

The truth is that both of us have had periods of significant disillusionment with the institutional church, and we are very distressed by the failure of so many congregations to extend true hospitality to each other and to those outside the church. We offer this book with the prayer that it can have a positive impact on your life, regardless of your involvement in a faith-based institution. God and God's love are not limited by the institutional structures of religion in our society.

Both of us are personally committed to the renewal of the church in our time. Fred works at that renewal as the continuing pastor of the rapidly growing congregation that provided much of the basis for our previous book together and through the hospitality workshops he conducts around the country. Steve works at that renewal through research, program development, writing, and consultation. Both of us find our lives richly blessed by friends both inside and outside the institutional church.

Biblical hospitality has in fact been a tremendous benefit to both of our lives–indeed, it has transformed us. We don't promise that you will agree with every word that follows; but we do promise that growth in the practice of hospitality has the power to positively impact almost every area of life. Read the book, study the concepts (by yourself or with others), and incorporate those concepts into your daily life–building a foundation of prayer and action which will bring you closer to God, closer to other people, and closer to the best in yourself.

Steve and Fred

Safety Tips
for
Hotel Guests

- Never open the door to your room without verifying who is there. All hotel employees wear picture IDs and uniforms.

- When you are in the room, keep the door closed and use both the bolt lock and the chain lock.

- Never invite strangers into your room.

- Avoid drawing attention by showing large amounts of cash or jewelry.

- Use the hotel's safe deposit box for jewelry and expensive equipment.

- Don't give other people your guest room number.

- Don't leave your key out on a restaurant table or at the swimming pool.

- Always keep the door to any connecting room closed and bolted.

- Call the assistant manager on duty if you see any suspicious activity.

- Never leave valuables in your automobile.

Chapter One
Fear and Loneliness

Concept: We live in a fearful time and have learned to lock our cars, homes, hearts, and minds. God offers us freedom from fear and the ability to make a difference in our world.

At one o'clock in the morning, Steve went to a 24-hour drugstore to get an allergy prescription refilled. He had forgotten to do it earlier in the day and knew he would need it before conducting a workshop that started at eight o'clock. A workshop leader with a drippy nose does not inspire confidence!

A woman named Mable, in her late seventies, was the only other customer at the prescription counter. She and Steve had a brief conversation in which he learned that she also had forgotten to get a prescription refilled earlier in the day, but hers was for high blood pressure. After she left, the pharmacist quickly took care of Steve's prescription.

When Steve returned to the parking lot, he found that Mable was still trying to get into her car. Two young adult males were hassling her by lightly slapping at the keys as she attempted to put them in the lock of her car. They kept calling her "Mama" and asking her to give them some money. It appeared that they weren't intending to actually steal her purse but rather hoped to intimidate her into a "donation."

Since there was a security guard in the store, Steve went inside and asked him for help. He responded by saying, "Oh, some of those young kids have a knife or a gun. It isn't safe to get involved. I'll give the police a call." Steve was perplexed, thinking that the security guard had a gun and was presumably there to keep customers safe.

Knowing that Mable had high blood pressure and had to be under horrible stress, Steve said a quick prayer and headed back to the parking lot. He approached Mable and the two young adults, saying to them, "Hey, come on, knock it off." They stepped away from Mable and gave their attention to Steve, who was counting on the fact that most bullies lose their bluster quickly when confronted. They exchanged a few more words, some of which are X-rated, and then the young adults took off when Steve reminded them that the police had been called.

Fifteen minutes later, the police still had not arrived. Steve and Mable were sitting in her car talking. She finally said, "Well, I think I feel calm enough to drive now. This is the first time in my life I've truly felt in danger. My friends keep telling me that things are different and that it isn't safe to be out after dark, but I don't want to live my life governed by fear. That's just no way to live."

Governed by Fear?

Millions of people in North America join Mable in wanting to lead lives that aren't governed by fear. The truth of the matter, however, is that fear plays a major part in the way that many of us live. Variations on the "Safety Tips for Hotel Guests" (found opposite the title page for this chapter) are found in hotel rooms around the world. Many of us don't feel safe in parking lots at night, in hotel rooms, or even in our homes. The presence of a security guard or a police officer helps some of us feel safe, but there are persons of non-white ethnic background who do not find the presence of a police officer particularly reassuring. Also there are not enough police officers to enable us to feel safe all the time. The police who seemed slow to respond to the call from the security guard were in fact responding to another crisis in a different neighborhood at the time.

While we are intrigued by experiences like the one of Steve and Mable, such events are in fact not as common place as the media and politicians would have us believe. The truth is that fears about crime and safety make good news stories and provide wonderful forums for platitudes and promises from politicians. That doesn't mean that some of the dangers aren't real, but we need to recognize the reality that powerful interests are served by causing us not to feel safe. Some of the newspaper headlines on the day Steve was writing his part of this chapter included:

LOCAL MAN KILLS THREE

14 TREATED FOR FIREWORKS INJURIES

GERMAN NAZI REPARATIONS COME TOO LATE

SENATOR FEARS HISTORY IMPEDES PEACE

STARR SPOKESMAN TO STAND TRIAL

PENTAGON PREPARES FOR MISSILE TRIAL

27 KILLED IN SPAIN COLLISION

HIJACKER HID GRENADE IN KIDS' BAGS

BELFAST TENSION HIGH AS MARCH PLANNED

There was also plenty of good news to report, but the most prominent headlines were ones reminding us how dangerous a place the world can be. Some local news shows have started segments with titles like "Focus on the Positive" and "Good News Spotlight." The very presence of those relatively short segments is a statement about the tone of much of the rest of the newscasts. Many of us lead more fearful lives than we realize.

While conducting a workshop on hospitality, Fred spent a delightful weekend as the guest of a couple who had a home on the side of a mountain. These were people of very high church involvement. Both of them have been volunteered in church sponsored disaster relief work and have traveled considerable distances to help people who are victims of floods, hurricanes, tornadoes, earthquakes, and fires.

They frequently open their home to guests who are present for church business in the area, and they are well known for their hospitality. Yet they have double-locked doors at both entrances to their house, and it takes two keys to get inside. Rather than a traditional screen door, they have a wrought iron door and then the main door. They keep their home locked all the time, even when there themselves during daylight hours.

During the workshop, Fred talked about the role that fear plays in our lives. One of his hosts attended the workshop, and he and Fred shared in some interesting dialogue as a result. There are not many break-ins or crimes in the area in which this couple lives; but like large numbers of people in contemporary North America, security has become a major issue to them. They live in fear of someone invading their space.

During the same workshop, Fred asked the guests how safe they feel and what is happening in terms of crime where they live. People have the perception that there is a high danger of their cars, homes, and businesses being robbed; and they are very concerned about the possibility of being assaulted.

Their geographical area, however, has a very low crime rate. People in the workshop had very little personal experience of any kind of crime. One person had seen a person siphoning gas off a van in an office parking lot, but that was the only specific, recent instance of criminal activity that any of the ninety workshop participants could identify.

Fred has asked people about how safe they feel, how often they lock their doors, and how high the crime rate really is in workshops all around North America. Of course one expects people in major urban areas such as Chicago, Los Angeles, or Toronto to be concerned about crime and to keep their doors locked all the time. Fred has been surprised, however, to discover that the habits of people are little different even in relatively small towns with very high church-going populations. Many people in Harrisonburg, Virginia, Orrville, Ohio, and Goshen, Indiana, are just as obsessed with keeping doors locked as people in far more urban areas.

What Do We Fear?

The purpose of this book isn't to persuade you to abandon caution, to frequent parking lots late at night, or to leave your car and home unlocked. What we want to do is explore with you some of the ways in which fear and loneliness impact our lives and to consider the spiritual basis for a different view of other people and of the world.

Take just a few moments to go through the list which follows and to rate your concern about each item from one to five with one representing "almost no fear at all" and five representing "a high level of fear."

____ 1.   Having my identity stolen through someone getting my credit card number and social security number.

____ 2.   Having my pocket picked or my purse snatched.

____ 3.   Having my car stolen.

____ 4.   Having my car broken into.

____ 5.   Being a victim of an armed robbery.

____ 6.   Having a burglary in my home while I'm gone.

____ 7.   Having a burglary in my home while I'm there.

____ 8.   Having my child or a child I know be kidnapped.

____ 9.   Being assaulted by another person.

____10. Having someone I love be assaulted.

____11. Being sexually assaulted.

____12. Having someone I love be sexually assaulted.

____13. Being cheated or taken advantage of by a stranger.

____14. Being cheated or taken advantage of by someone I trust.

____15. Having a heart attack, cancer, or another life-threatening illness.

____16. Having someone I love have a heart attack, cancer, or another life-threatening illness.

____18. Being injured by a drunken driver.

____19. Having someone I love be injured by a drunken driver.

____20. Having drinking water made unsafe by pollution.

____21. Having the air made unsafe by pollution.

____22. Having my descendants inherit a world without safe water and air.

____23. Ending up without enough money to take care of myself in later years.

____24. Not having enough money to take care of those I love.

___25. Being in the midst of a tornado.

___26. Being in the midst of a hurricane.

___27. Losing my home to a fire.

___28. Hurting someone by being careless in driving.

___29. Making bad financial decisions which cause serious problems for my family.

___30. Failing to respond to the needs of others as God would have me respond.

___31. Failing to do what God wants me to with my life.

___32. Dying and finding that I have disappointed God.

___33. Losing loved ones to death and still having years to go by myself.

___34. Doing something that loses the confidence my friends and family have in me.

___35. Finding I have been betrayed by a loved one.

___36. Becoming permanently disabled.

___37. Having a loved one become permanently disabled.

___38. Disappointing my employer or employees.

___39. Getting in trouble with the Internal Revenue Service.

___40. Being accused of a crime of which I'm not guilty.

___41. Having violence at a school in my community.

___42. Having a child of mine or one I know be harmed by drugs or alcohol.

___43. Looking foolish to other people.

___44. Appearing pathetic or lonely to other people.

___45. Looking like I can't control my emotions.

Obviously the list could be significantly expanded. Your greatest fears may or may not be represented in those forty-five items. Try going through the list again and rating each item in terms of how likely you think it is to actually happen. There may well be some items on the list that have already happened to you and which have had significant impact on your life.

Bad things in fact do happen to us. The world is not always a safe place, and no book or politician is going to make it safe. But how fearfully do we really want to live?

Fear and Loneliness

We have all experienced rejection because we were strangers to others. We know what it feels like to be ordered to present a driver's license and a credit card to get a check accepted at a store.

We know the fear of having car trouble on the highway and not having anyone stop. We know the anxiety of trying to find our way around an unfamiliar neighborhood or city. In all these situations, we feel a fundamental loneliness.

In many respects, fear and distrust seem to have spread like a cancer in our land. Symbols of openness are disappearing from the North American scene as we barricade ourselves from strangers in an effort to protect ourselves and our possessions. Electric door locks on cars, double locks on house doors, security alarms, guard dogs, lobby guards, security officers, increased numbers of police, and the military are just a few signs of our deeply held fear of the stranger. We hide our money, lock our doors, chain our bikes, and look over our shoulders.

News reports of break-ins, break-outs, and blackouts feed our fears. We have come to view strangers more as potential enemies than as potential friends. We keep our eyes on our luggage and pocketbooks as we travel. We may feel sympathy for the hitchhiker or the stranded motorist, but most of the time we keep driving. When we park in a shopping mall lot, we lock our valuables in the trunk, away from the eyes of strangers. We are often victimized by our fears, instinctively avoiding persons who look or speak differently than we do.

All our social institutions have been affected by the growth of fear in our society. Churches, once known as havens of refuge and houses of prayer, now lock the doors to the very persons to whom they claim to minister. Our schools now post guards to protect students from students and teachers from students. Drug-sniffing dogs and metal detectors have become standard operating procedure in many schools. Many office buildings and large companies have significantly increased security, with some requiring registration of everyone who enters.

Certainly the statistics on violent crime over the past two decades justify a somewhat cautious approach to certain situations. Yet it is one thing to live with a reasonable sense of caution and another entirely to have most of one's existence determined by fear. Instead of risking new possibilities for ourselves and the stranger, too many of us continue hiding behind our walls, lamenting the world's condition. By failing to come to know the stranger, we too often make that person an enemy rather than a friend.

That tendency has fed our loneliness. Large numbers of people feel shut off from others. People are cautious in new relationships, wanting to feel safe before revealing much of themselves or trusting too much in the other person.

Our loneliness is also fed by the technology of our time. E-mail has rapidly become one of the most frequently used means of communication, and in many respects it is a tremendous blessing. In certain respects, however, e-mail is a significantly less personal means of communication than a phone call or a face-to-face conversation.

Increasing numbers of people find that they can comfortably work out of their homes. Steve does most of his work at a desk in the study of his home. E-mail, the fax machine, Federal Express, and the telephone enable him to stay strongly connected to those with whom he works. He and his colleagues in the Christian Community and LifeQuest organizations often exchange manuscript files and research data files by attachments to e-mail.

It's a very effective means of sharing information, and it makes it possible to work easily with people hundreds or even thousands of miles away.

Steve's work also involves considerable travel and face-to-face interactions with his coworkers and others, so he continually feels strongly connected with people. It's easy to see, however, how the same style of work at home, for a person who did not travel much, could lead to a sense of isolation. The technology, on the whole, is a great blessing, but we need to be aware of the ways in which it can also feed loneliness.

A young adult who recently moved five hundred miles away from his home to accept a new job shared this perspective: "I'm surrounded by people, but I've never felt so lonely. There are two hundred people in the office where I work, and I know at least thirty of them by name already. But I don't do anything with them outside of work. I'm the new one in the department, and the others already have friends and a social life. People are nice to me, but I feel on the outside looking in.

"There are some people in the company that I only know through e-mail exchange and an occasional phone conversation. They work in other parts of the building or in another branch of the company, and there just isn't any occasion for us to get together. Sometimes I think about suggesting a face-to-face meeting with people in the same building, but then I think that would sound pretty needy.

"I live in a good-sized apartment complex, maybe eighty apartments and a couple of hundred people. The reality is that my neighbors don't talk to each other. There are a few who make eye contact and smile, but they feel like the exception. I never thought of myself as introverted, but I don't know how to start getting to know people.

"I visited a couple of churches. I was the only young adult at both of them. I didn't especially mind that. People were friendly on the surface. The greeters and ushers shook hands with me, and visitors were introduced in the worship service at one of the churches. But people didn't remember who I was when I return-ed the next week.

"I know it will come in time, but right now I'm very sorry that I moved here. I thought that I needed a new beginning away from my family and my college friends, but I'm not so sure now."

Then consider these comments from a woman who is eighty-two years old and has lived in the same neighborhood for the last forty-five years: "Everything in my life has changed in the last two decades. My husband has been dead for eight years now, but I'm still not adjusted to living alone. Every squeak in the house bothers me. My cat should be named Big Foot because he can sound just like a person coming up the stairs in the middle of the night.

"The whole neighborhood has changed. I know the names of the people on either side of me, and they seem like nice enough people. The young couple on one side of me makes a point every so often of saying, 'Now, you just call us if you need something.' I think they're sincere, and they'd help me get to the hospital in the middle of the night. But I can't call them just to say that I feel lonely. That would make me feel so foolish.

"It seems like my friends in the community and in the organizations I belong to keep moving into retirement homes or dying. I've been to four funerals this year. Each one makes me wonder how much longer I'll live, but I seem to keep going. My diabetes is under control, and my arthritis doesn't bother me as much as it seems to a lot of other people.

"But I'm in danger of outliving everyone who is important to me. And it's just not easy to make new friends, especially at my age."

Not all the fears that feed loneliness are big fears of crime or being taken advantage of by others. Some of the fears that affect us are more difficult to identify and sometimes awkward to acknowledge:

- The fear of appearing needy to others.

- The fear of others knowing how lonely we feel.

- The fear that others will not like us because of our age, appearance, economic status, race, or lifestyle.

- The fear of appearing foolish to others.

- The fear of acknowledging our own need for others.

Hospitality

The word hospitality is not new. We practice it in various ways as part of everyday life. At times, especially with those we already know and trust or know through others, we model it almost perfectly. We speak of southern hospitality and understand the meaning of a "Hospitality Inn" sign. We use the word to describe persons who exhibit extraordinary graciousness. Being hospitable is for some the opposite of being rude. The word also evokes images of tea parties, pleasant conversations, and an aura of coziness.

The meaning and explanation of hospitality, however, go deeper than those images. The experience and practice of hospitality lies at the very core of what it means to be a person of faith in the Christian or Jewish tradition. An old Hebrew proverb notes that "hospitality to strangers is greater than reverence for the name of God" [Robert E. Meagher in "Stranger at the Gate" in *Parabola 2*].

In the New Testament, the **Letter to the Hebrews** emphasizes the importance of hospitality: "Do not neglect to show hospitality to strangers, for by doing that some have entertained angels without knowing it" [13:2].

In our book *Widening the Welcome of the Church*, we defined hospitality and the stranger in this way:

> **Hospitality** is the **attitude** and **practice** of providing
> the **atmosphere** and **opportunities**, however risky,
> in which strangers are free to become friends, thereby
> feeling accepted, included, and loved. The relationship
> thus opens up the possibility for eventual communion
> among the host, the stranger, and God.

> The **stranger** is any person or group not known

to the host. The host perceives that this unknown
person or group has the potential for relationship
as an enemy or as a friend.

Those definitions focused especially on the life of the church as the body of Christ and on the way in which hospitality should be practiced within congregational life. In this book, we want to move the discussion of hospitality out of the context of the congregation and into the very heart of the spiritual life for each of us. Consider this definition, as shared in the introduction:

Hospitality involves recognizing the presence of Christ in family, friends, coworkers, neighbors, and complete strangers. It means responding to others as we would respond to the presence of Christ in our midst.

The answer to fear is not to be found in the locks on our doors, in the promises of politicians, in increased police forces or prison populations, or in changed reporting by the news media. The answer to loneliness is not to be found in personal ads, in singles bars, in retirement communities, or in assertiveness training.

The answer to the fear and loneliness of our time comes in the development of the spiritual life and in a new way of seeing the people with whom we share our existence. Hospitality, fundamentally, is not a program for the church or even for self-improvement. It is a different way of living that sets us free to love and to be loved.

Programs and resources can, of course, help us in the

development of a greater hospitality as individuals, as congregations, and as other organizations of people. We've been pleased by the way many congregations have had their hospitality improved through a careful study of *Widening the Welcome of Your Church* and through the initiation of new policies. We trust that reading *Hospitality: Life without Fear* will help many people at an individual level and also that it will help congregations and other organizations in society. The core changes needed remain at the spiritual level. True hospitality is a matter of faith.

> *Fear knocked at the door.*
> *Faith answered.*
> *No one was there.*

Some Facts about Guns

- Every two hours in the United States, someone's child is killed with a loaded gun.

- If there is a gun in the home, the risk of suicide is five times greater.

- If there is a gun in the home, the risk of domestic homicide is three times greater.

- Over 50% of handgun owners keep their guns loaded, and over 50% do not keep their guns locked up.

- Firearms are often kept at home for protection, but they are seldom used for that purpose. Only 1.5% of those persons who were victims of home invasion crimes used a gun for self-defense.

- In 1998, of the 61 police officers who were murdered in the line of duty, 58 were killed with firearms. Six police officers were murdered with their own service weapons.

- There are over 200 million firearms in North America.

- A safety on a gun is a mechanical device–it can fail. Long guns are not "drop safe" even if they have safeties. The safety of a long gun normally blocks only the trigger but not the firing pin or the hammer.

Based on 1999 and 2000 information from the National Rifle Association and from United States Uniform Crime Reporting statistics.

Chapter Two
The Spiritual Life and Hospitality

> **Concept:** Hospitality is not another self-improvement program. True hospitality is rooted in the spiritual life and transforms the way we view ourselves, other people, and God.

Melanie is a 28 year-old editor who loves mountain climbing. She grew up in Phoenix, Arizona, and learned from her father and her friends how to climb while a teenager. Now that she lives in New York City, mountains are not as easy to find; but she plans her vacations and an occasional long weekend to get as much climbing opportunity as possible. She has a special savings account to finance a trip to Mount Everest in three years.

She says that she would actually try scaling a couple of the skyscrapers in New York City, but local laws are designed to discourage such activities. She could climb a skyscraper and end up with a stiff fine and some bad publicity for her employer, both of which seem like too high a price for her.

"I don't actually think of it as dangerous," she says in describing her passion. "I've been climbing for so many years that I know my limitations, and I know the importance of doing it with people I trust. My boyfriend, who would like to be my fiancé, does feel that it's dangerous, though he's taken it up partly because it's so important to me and partly because he likes risk.

"It is more dangerous for him, because he's not as skilled as I am and doesn't always know his limitations. For him a lot of it is because he wants to share the experience with me, but it's also his own desire to overcome his fear. He was almost scared to death the first few times we simply scaled a wall at a big sporting goods store. But overcoming fear is important to him.

"He'd been bungee jumping and sky diving before we met. Now those, to me, really sound dangerous. You're like totally dependent on your equipment. One mistake–you're a mashed potato. The equipment is important in mountain climbing; but I think you have a lot more control over what happens to you than in some other extreme sports. So I'm not scared of climbing, but there is no way you would get me to jump out of an airplane."

When asked why she does it, Melanie responded: "It's become part of me, part of my identity. I love the experience, the adrenalin rush, the beauty of being that high. I also like doing it with other people, the kind of bond you develop with others as you climb together. That's something I don't think you get from bungee jumping or sky diving, not in the same kind of way. And there's actually a spiritual dimension for me–there's a sense in which climbing makes me feel connected with the natural world and with God. My uncle is a Presbyterian minister, and he and I have talked about some of the ways being connected with nature, with the earth, makes us more connected with God. I don't say that to most people, but that's part of what I feel."

We seek experiences that transcend our everyday lives in a multitude of ways. Interest in what are sometimes called extreme sports has risen significantly over the last decade. Participation has increased significantly in mountain climbing, bungee jumping, sky diving, downhill mountain biking, and boxing. Some adventurous people like BASE jumping which involves parachuting off fixed objects like radio towers and bridges. BASE stands for Buildings, Antennas, Spans, and Earth!

The Sporting Goods Manufacturers Association says that in 1996, the fastest-growing sport among teens and children in North America was in-line skating, which often means zooming down steep hills at speeds of 30 or 40 miles an hour. While not quite in the same category, hockey has enjoyed a tremendous increase in participation with amateur leagues appearing in cities around North America.

Not everyone who climbs mountains would call the experience spiritual, but Melanie's response is also not an unusual one. Many people, working at jobs that involve primarily their minds, crave opportunities that challenge them physically and that involve them emotionally at a deeper level than everyday life.

Melanie doesn't think of climbing as dangerous in the way that many people, including the authors of this book, would. She does acknowledge that a certain amount of fear is healthy. Fear can be what motivates you to be sure your equipment is in good condition, to be sure you are well informed about weather, and to be sure you climb with people who are trustworthy. Too much fear can immobilize us, but a reasonable amount for rational reasons can keep us safe.

A young adult in the Army loved sky diving, but he also maintained that he would quit when he was no longer scared. He had observed that people who lose their fear with repetition sometimes start to get careless. That's when accidents happen, and sky diving accidents are fatal. When he reached the point that he was no longer frightened by these experiences, he stopped.

Seeking Experience and Meaning

We seek experience and meaning in a multitude of ways. Sports, travel, sex, drugs, and friendship can all be means of transcending our normal existence. There is in fact a hunger within us which pulls us to experiences that involve our bodies and our emotions as well as our minds. Many of us, however, do not seek to develop the spiritual life with the same energy that we put into gaining an education, earning a living, participating in sports, or even keeping the house clean. Thus the spiritual life becomes one part of who we are, but not the center of our being.

Much of the reason we are so driven by fear in our culture, that we are so uneasy around strangers, is that the spiritual life is not the main factor determining how we view other people and the opportunities available to us. We keep the spiritual life on the sidelines, ready to come into play if we attend a worship service or have a major crisis in our lives, but we don't develop it in such a way that it shapes how we live on a daily basis.

In calling this book *Hospitality: Life without Fear*, we aren't intending to say that fear has no place at all in one's life. The concepts presented in this book are designed to liberate you from *unhealthy* fear. We all need to be free of the fear that blocks and distorts the quality of our relationships with others and that makes us view the world around us with suspicion and lack of trust. That fear damages relationships with others and keeps us from viewing the world as God views it. There is another kind of fear that can be healthy, and that is the fear of God. Consider these verses of Scripture:

The fear of the LORD is the beginning of wisdom;
all those who practice it have a good understanding.
                                        Psalm 111:10

The fear of the LORD is the beginning of wisdom,
and the knowledge of the Holy One is insight.
                                        Proverbs 9:10

Commit your work to the LORD, and your plans
will be established. . . . By loyalty and faithfulness
iniquity is atoned for, and by the fear of the LORD
one avoids evil."
                                        Proverbs 16:3, 6

The spirit of the LORD shall rest on him, the spirit
of wisdom and understanding, the spirit of counsel
and might, the spirit of knowledge and the fear of the
LORD. His delight shall be in the fear of the LORD.
                                        Isaiah 11:2, 3a

Jehoshaphat gave this warning to judges: *"Now, let*
the fear of the LORD be upon you; take care what you
do, for there is no perversion of justice with the LORD
our God, or partiality, or taking of bribes."
                                        2 Chronicles 19:7

---

*Do not fear those who kill the body but cannot kill
the soul; rather fear him who can destroy both soul
and body in hell.*

Matthew 10:28

*His mercy is for those who fear him from generation
to generation.*

Luke 1:50

*Meanwhile the church throughout Judea, Galilee, and
Samaria had peace and was built up. Living in the
fear of the Lord and in the comfort of the Holy Spirit,
it increased in numbers.*

Acts 9:31

Of course the word fear has a variety of meanings in those
passages. We are not commanded to live in an immobilizing fear
but rather to live out of a desire to know and to do God's will.
The fear of God is closely linked to love of God and obedience to
God.

In **First John 4:17–20**, we are promised that perfect love
casts out fear, but perfect love is also directly related to how we
view other people:

*God is love, and those who abide in love abide in God,
and God abides in them. Love has been perfected among
us in this: that we may have boldness on the day of
judgment, because as he is, so are we in this world.
There is no fear in love, but perfect love casts out
fear; for fear has to do with punishment, and whoever
fears has not reached perfection in love. We love*

40

because he first loved us. Those who say "I love God,"
and hate their brothers or sisters, are liars; for those
who do not love a brother or sister whom they have
seen, cannot love God whom they have not seen.

We are still striving for perfection in love, but most of us (at least in the experience of the authors) have not reached that goal. Thus a healthy fear of God, a genuine desire to know and do the will of God, should play a part in our spiritual lives. And that healthy fear of God, which motivates us to see the world differently, can transform our relationships with others. The search for meaning and experience is ultimately a search for God, who can be found on the mountaintops as Melanie does, but who can also be found within our hearts and around our lives each day of our existence. And the presence of God is continually coming to us in the strangers we encounter.

Lover of Strangers

The Greek word which is translated as hospitality, *philoxenos*, literally means "lover of strangers," which is similar to the Greek *philadelphia* or brotherly love. The concept of loving strangers is a foreign one to most of us. Far more of us have learned to be suspicious of strangers than to hold strangers in affection.

On a long airline flight, Fred met a delightful thirty-nine year old man who had grown up in the Jewish faith. Fred is normally the one to take the initiative in starting conversations with strangers, but this fellow traveler was the one to initiate their visit. He was fascinated to learn that Fred was a minister, and he shared with Fred that he had become a non-practicing Jew except for holy days. When Fred told him about the hospitality workshop that he was traveling to conduct, his new friend shared that his father had been the head usher in his childhood temple on Long Island. His father made sure visitors found a place to sit and people with whom to visit. His father would also see that these people received an invitation for a meal and a place to stay if needed.

Some of the spirit of that hospitality has obviously continued in this non-practicing Jew. He's on the board of a ski lodge, and he feels that he has a responsibility when at the lodge to help people feel at home. He also practices hospitality in a less traditional, and some would even say less safe, way: he travels a lot and always picks up hitch-hikers and tries to help them with food or money if needed.

Fred asked him why he picks up hitch-hikers, something that most people are frightened to do. He responded, "Because it's the decent, human thing to do." Fred suggested to him that his motivation may run deeper than he realizes: it may relate to his faith experiences early in life and to the example set by his father. Fred talked with him about hospitality from a biblical point of view and about Abraham as the patron saint of hospitality. Fred's new friend immediately identified with Abraham and remembered teachings from Hebrew School as he grew up.

When they arrived at their destination, the man accepted Fred's card and said to him, "You are the first person in a long time I've been able to talk with about life issues–about what really matters. It seems like the conversations of my life are almost always just skimming along the surface."

Many of the conversations of life do skim along the surface, but Fred's Jewish friend is not alone in the desire to discover greater depth. Both he and Fred were blessed by their encounter on the plane. The Old Testament and the New Testament make it clear that strangers can be the source of great blessings.

Fred referred to Abraham as the patron saint of hospitality. **Genesis 18:1-15** describes one of the most significant instances of Abraham's hospitality. Three strangers appear at the entrance of Abraham's tent, and he responds to them in a gracious manner. Biblical scholars (including Vawter, Von Rad, and Fretheim) agree that the three strangers are personages of Yahweh, though we are not clear in precisely what way. In *The New Interpreter's Bible*, Terence Fretheim offers this perspective: "From the narrator's point of view, Yahweh appears to Abraham at his home (v.1). From Abraham's point of view, however, three men stand near him (v.2). Yahweh has assumed human form appearing among the three men; the other two are angelic attendants" [Volume I, pp. 462-463]. Consider the text:

> *The Lord appeared to Abraham by the oaks of Mamre,*
> *as he sat at the entrance of his tent in the heat of the*
> *day. He looked up and saw three men standing near*
> *him. When he saw them, he ran from the tent entrance*
> *to meet them, and bowed down to the ground. He said,*
> *"My lord, if I find favor with you, do not pass by your*
> *servant. Let a little water be brought, and wash your*
> *feet, and rest yourselves under the tree. Let me bring*
> *a little bread, that you may refresh yourselves, and*
> *after that you may pass on—since you have come to*
> *your servant."*

---

*So they said, "Do as you have said." And Abraham
hastened into the tent to Sarah, and said, "Make ready
quickly three measures of choice flour, knead it, and
make cakes." Abraham ran to the herd, and took a
calf, tender and good, and gave it to the servant, who
hastened to prepare it. Then he took curds and milk
and the calf that he had prepared, and set it before them;
and he stood by them under the tree while they ate.*
Genesis 18:1-8

Abraham offers hospitality without being aware of the divine presence. That hospitality is consistent with the practice in the Ancient Near East and includes these elements:

- Abraham bows to them.

- Abraham offers them water, rest, and food.

- They accept.

- The meal is prepared and includes a calf, which would have been reserved for a special occasion, and butter, which was greatly prized by the nomad.

- Abraham waits on them while they eat.

- The strangers did not reveal their identity nor did they offer any gift or payment prior to the meal.

In sharing the calf and the butter, Abraham and Sarah gave far more than custom required. They chose to treat the three men as honored guests, and they did so without expecting anything in return. In verses 9-15, one of them tells Sarah that she will have a son. The fact that the gift of a child was promised can be seen as a response to their hospitality, but the promise of a son had already been made in the preceding chapter. The hospitality existed for its own sake, and Abraham has been lifted up as a model because of it. Had Abraham and Sarah refused hospitality to the strangers, they would have shut themselves off from the blessings God intended–not just the blessing of a son but also the blessing of God's presence.

The familiar New Testament words of **Hebrews 13:2** are likely a reference to Abraham's experience: "Do not neglect to show hospitality to strangers, for by doing that some have entertained angels without knowing it." The New Testament provides us with a very strong example of hospitality in the parable of the Good Samaritan as recorded in **Luke 10:29-37**. The Samaritan did not evaluate the risk in responding to the person in need. The response was immediate, and it is a standard for our conduct–Jesus tells us to "Go and do likewise" [v. 37b].

The Presence of Christ

Matthew 25:31-46 presents an account very similar in some ways to that in Genesis 18. We are told to reach out to those who are hungry, naked, homeless, or imprisoned. When we show hospitality to such persons, it is as though the kindness was actually being shown to Christ:

> *"Lord, when was it that we saw you hungry or thirsty or a stranger or naked or sick or in prison, and did not take care of you?"*

> *Then he will answer them, "Truly I tell you, just as you
> did not do it to one of the least of these, you did not do it
> to me"* [25:45-46].

Fred likes to call Jesus the "Supreme Hospitalitor," for he laid
down his life for others. The intention in Matthew 25 is to show
the certainty of the end time and to answer the question of who
will be judged as righteous. Persons who are hospitable to
strangers are credited with those deeds as if the other person were
Jesus Christ himself.

In this passage, Jesus makes it clear that we are not to reject
the needy stranger like the son of man who was rejected and
crucified. The stranger is to be welcomed, accepted, fed, and
clothed. Welcoming the stranger opens the door to building
relationships and developing deeper communion with one another
and with God. Our relationships with others are transformed
when we seriously consider the reality that we are encountering
Christ in the other person. That should affect all of our
relationships, every day of our lives.

The presence of Christ in others, of course, can be seen even
more clearly in long term relationships; and we rightly cherish our
parents, spouses, children, grandchildren, grandparents, and close
friends. All of our closest friends, however, were once strangers
to us. Recognizing Christ in others does not require a large set of
shared experiences, though those experiences, clearly seen and
understood, certainly deepen our bonds with others.

In *Reaching Out*, Henri Nouwen describes a visit from a
person who had previously been a student in one of his courses.
They sat on the ground together to talk, and then chose to sit in

silence for a time. Nouwen felt a deep peace filling the space between them, and then his visitor said: "When I look at you it is as if I am in the presence of Christ."

Nouwen did not feel startled but simply replied: "It is the Christ in you, who recognizes the Christ in me."

"Yes," the visitor responded, "He indeed is in our midst." Then the visitor went on to speak words which Nouwen said were the most healing that had entered his soul in many years:

> *From now on, wherever you go, or wherever I go,*
> *all the ground between us will be holy ground* [p. 31].

The distance between ourselves and others begins to be transformed when we view it as holy ground, when we truly recognize the presence of Christ in all those with whom we share our days: family members, long-time friends, coworkers, neighbors, and strangers. The stranger in our lives today may be a long-time friend years later; or we may never again see the stranger, who nevertheless is a source of blessings to us.

Those of the Quaker heritage sometimes speak of the divine spark in each person's breast. When we are open to the presence of that spark, it ignites and gains its own life. That spark is present even if we do not recognize it and even if we are afraid to name it as God within us. Others are more comfortable talking about the Holy Spirit as the divine presence within our hearts. Whatever name we place on the reality, that presence is in our hearts, in the hearts of those we have known for years, and in the hearts of those who have only this day come into our lives.

Some people who show hospitality are like Fred's traveling friend in not relating those acts of kindness to a spiritual motivation. The instruction of our childhood may affect our view of the world and our actions more deeply than we realize. At other times, the Christ within us, the Holy Spirit, the divine spark, may move us to great hospitality even though we fail to recognize the source of the desire to act in a loving way. The nonreligious can and do come to hospitality because of that unrecognized divine presence. It is possible to love one's neighbor without loving God, but God is nevertheless at the root of that love. If we crave a heightened spiritual life, then we need to open ourselves more fully to the presence of Christ within our lives. We then need to seek Christ's help in recognizing his presence in the lives of others, including the lives of strangers.

Guns to Ease Our Fears

But we are not accustomed to seeing Christ in the lives of strangers. Our fear of strangers and of crime continues to fuel a prosperous firearms industry. Most people who purchase guns for protection rather than for hunting would prefer not to be in a situation in which the gun had to be used, but the news media and other forces at work in our society have caused them to feel unsafe without a weapon. The information about guns, opposite the first page of this chapter, provides some reminders of the consequences of our placing reliance on firearms for protection.

We recognize that there will be many good people reading these words who take the faith seriously and who own handguns. Please consider the possibility that the weapon you have may end up used in a way you never intended. Firearms in fact are seldom used at home for protection, although many are purchased for that purpose. They are more likely to be used in three terrifying ways:

- As the cause of death for a child. Children do not understand firearms and are very curious about them. Television and motion pictures often depict violence in a way that is significantly different than real life. And children have an ability to find hidden firearms without parents realizing it until too late. Having a gun at the back of the top shelf of a closet isn't being safe enough. Even very young children find ways to climb. Having the weapon unloaded doesn't make it safe if there is anyway a child can find ammunition, and 50% of hand-gun owners keep their weapons loaded. Every two hours in the United States, a child is killed with a loaded gun.

- As the means of suicide. Statistical evidence continues to show that the risk of suicide is five times greater if there is a gun in the house. Obviously people take their own lives in a variety of ways besides firearms, but the ready availability and ease of use of a handgun increase the probability of someone taking that step.

- As the means of domestic homicide. Tragically, most people are in greater danger of violence from those they know and love than from strangers. The risk of domestic homicide is three times greater when there is a gun in the home. When feelings run strong and a gun is readily available, the temptation is more than some people can resist.

The statistics on guns we've shared at the start of this chapter and in this section come from 1999 and 2000 information from the National Rifle Association and from United States Uniform Crime Reporting data. The National Rifle Association argues persuasively that, if people are going to own guns, they need to be trained in how to safely store them and use them. The authors of this book have no argument with that and have respect for the educational work of the National Rifle Association.

But there is a more fundamental question which most of us need to ask: Do we need guns at all? If we are not hunters, why own a gun? Most of us do not have streets or neighborhoods that are so dangerous we need to be armed at all times. The presence of the gun is not very likely to protect us. The gun is far more likely to injure our children or grandchildren, to be the means by which a suicide is committed, or to be utilized in domestic violence.

Most police officers are considerably more knowledgeable and experienced in the use of firearms than most gun owners. Yet in 1998, six of the 58 police officers in the United States who were killed by firearms *were killed with their own service weapons.* If police officers, who are highly trained and experienced, are that likely to be murdered by their own weapons, what does that say about the probability of the rest of us being harmed by our own guns?

One person who read this manuscript before publication made this observation: "This is a very strong argument against handguns, but what are the alternatives to help people feel safe if they do not have guns?" That is a fundamental question, and we cannot tell you that you will be safe from harm if you do not have a handgun. We do hope the information in this book will cause you to think carefully about the issues involved in owning a gun. Our argument against handguns for people other than law enforcement officers is based on three things:

1. The conviction that, for most of us, the dangers of owning a handgun are greater than any potential protection provided by the weapon.

2. The conviction that the world, while not entirely safe, is not as dangerous as news media, motion pictures, television programs, politicians, and others have caused us to feel. Reasonable precautions such as locks, alarm systems, and care in our routines can help protect us without bringing the danger of gun ownership.

3. The conviction that a deep spiritual life causes us to recognize the presence of Christ in others, including those we are tempted to fear. And a deeply held faith means that we ultimately depend upon God for our protection, knowing our Lord is with us no matter what we encounter.

Christ is in our spouses, parents, children, grandparents, and grandchildren. Christ is in our neighbors. Christ is even in the teenager who breaks into houses. How much danger are we willing to cause for others as the price for the security we feel from owning a handgun?

Help Me, Please

Hank, an exhausted executive, didn't leave his downtown office until 8:30 p.m. on a cold February evening. As he approached the almost deserted parking lot, Hank noticed a man getting out of an older car. The man and the car seemed to match each other, both clearly having had better days before the dings, scrapes, and rust of life left their marks.

As Hank headed for his own car, the man limped toward him. Hank hurried his pace, and the stranger hurried his, calling to Hank, "Could you help me, please?"

Hank thought it might be a person simply seeking a handout but was afraid the man might try to steal his billfold when he got close. Choosing to ignore him, Hank increased his pace and tried to put confidence and determination into his walk. He used his remote control to unlock his car doors and turn on the lights, which immediately made him feel safer. He got into his car and locked the doors just before the stranger came even with him.

Looking up as the stranger tapped on his window, Hank reluctantly lowered his window an inch to hear what the man said. "Could you help me, please?"

"I don't think so," Hank responded. "I don't have any money with me, so there's nothing I can do for you."

"I don't want money," the stranger responded and smiled. "My car won't start. I think all I need is a jump, and I have cables in my trunk. I've asked three people to help, and they've all refused. I called a wrecker service about coming to give me a jump, but they said it would be at least another hour. Is there any chance you could help me out?"

At close distance, the man looked like a mess; but he didn't look like a dangerous mess. The previous month, Hank's wife had been stranded, in a supermarket parking lot, with a similar problem without any help for two hours. Hank decided to take a chance.

The jump was all that the old car needed. As Hank started to leave, the stranger extended his hand and said, "I forgot to introduce myself. I'm Father Bill. I work at an inner city mission about eight blocks from here. Unfortunately, no one on staff there could leave to help me."

"You're a priest?!" Hank, also a Catholic, said in amazement. "Why didn't you say so? Why aren't you wearing a collar? I'd have helped you immediately if I'd known who you were."

"Well," Father Bill responded with another smile, "I am a priest, but a collar is a turn off to many of the people I'm trying to help. A lot of them have had bad experiences with the church. But wouldn't I have been just as deserving of help if I were the freeloader you first took me to be? Christ might be more fully present in the freeloader than in me."

> *Do not neglect to show hospitality to strangers, for by doing that some have entertained angels without knowing it.*   Hebrews 32:2

Crime and Punishment

- If current incarceration rates in the United States remain unchanged, an estimated one out of every twenty people (5.1%) will serve time in a prison during his or her life.

- Based on current rates of incarceration, 28% of black males will enter a state or federal prison during their lifetime. The figure is 16% for Hispanic males and 4.4% for white males.

- Only 17% of federal inmates are in prison for a violent offense; 58% of them are imprisoned for a drug offense.

- 48% of jailed women reported having been physically or sexually abused prior to their incarceration.

- Over a third of all inmates report some kind of physical or mental disability.

- In 1996 and 1997, only a fourth of local jail inmates around North America were being held for a violent crime.

- 36% of convicted offenders were drinking alcohol at the time of the offense.

- Between 1980 and 1997, the population of California's state prisons increased by six times.

- It costs more to keep an inmate four years in a state or federal prison than to send the inmate to a private college.

1997, 1998, 1999 U.S. Department of Justice and State of California statistics.

Chapter Three
Our Need for ~~Strangers~~ Guests

> **Concept:** Our tendency to spend time only with those we already know limits us and keeps us from receiving all the blessings God offers. We need to see the unknown person not as a stranger but as a guest sent from God to enrich our lives.

Fred routinely makes new friends as he travels to conduct workshops and seminars. One of those new friends, Roberto, had lived for more than a year in an exclusive San Francisco suburb without knowing any of his neighbors by name. Roberto tried to strike up conversations with people, but he wasn't successful. It was a beautiful area in which to live, but people were cold toward one another.

Roberto wanted to live in a warmer, more friendly community, so he started looking for a complex that allowed pets. His theory was that people with pets would be more friendly and that there would be opportunities for conversation with people walking dogs. He was not disappointed with his new neighborhood! Pets constituted a safe topic for conversation; and the process of walking dogs provided many opportunities for interaction. People could sometimes move from the relatively safe topic of comparing pet experiences to talking about more personal things.

Animals, Nature, and People

Pets have a significant influence on many of our lives. Steve's Siamese cat, Tia, often sits on his desk, supervising his work. Often, a paw will gently touch his hand with the reminder that it's time to take a break from writing and share some affection with the supervisor.

When we encounter other people with pets, opportunities for conversation quickly open. We have an immediate point of connection; and at some level, many of us feel safer with people who have pets. It is as though the bond we form with pets and the gentleness required to make friends of them humanizes us in some important ways.

While pets can be quite demanding, sharing a home with a pet is less demanding than sharing a home with another person. Food, water, and affection are the main demands of a pet. Well, bathroom facilities are also important: litter boxes for cats, outdoor journeys for dogs, and other arrangements for more exotic creatures. At the date of this writing, there are reports of a new strategy for training dogs to use litter boxes, thus ending the necessity of walks; if that becomes a trend, it could have a negative impact on Roberto's social life.

Pets don't voice disagreements with us about religion, politics, motion pictures, or lifestyle issues. They don't chide us for overeating or undereating, and they never criticize us for failing to earn more money or for not attaining a higher status job. They don't aspire to a more upscale neighborhood, as they generally prefer to stay wherever we are right now. Most of them forgive us quickly when we treat them badly, and few of them harbor grudges. It's very difficult to maintain in any close human relationship the constancy of affection and devotion offered by a dog or a cat.

Our interest in animals extends beyond the domestic ones. Some of us feel more comfortable extending hospitality to animals than to people. We put out bird feeders and squirrel feeders, and we are delighted when we have a good response.

One can make a theological case for kindness to animals. Matthew Fox writes in *Confessions*:

> *Part of a Cosmic Christ theology is experiencing*
> *the Christ nature in all beings. I was gifted with*
> *such a friendship for seventeen years in the person*
> *of my dog, Tristan. . . . He was my spirit-guide*
> *for seventeen years, and after his death he has*
> *appeared in my dreams and those of others who*
> *knew him. I include him among a pantheon of spirits*
> *that have assisted me over the years.* [pp. 155-56]

Some readers may find it difficult to accept Fox's identification of a dog as a spirit guide. Yet pets have a calming influence on us and often cause us to be kinder people. They slow us down when we are too busy, and their very presence can remind us of our priorities in life. Is it too great a stretch to think of them as guides sent from God to help us improve our lives?

But obviously there are dangers in carrying this too far. Fred has had a number of intriguing conversations with people living in the beautiful Pacific Northwest who talk about experiencing God so much in nature that they have no interest in the community of the church. There are people who not only love pets but truly prefer the company of animals to the company of humans.

A great many of us, at times, may prefer the presence of animals to the presence of humans, especially at the end of a long, busy day. That's not the same as a life in which pets have actually become more important than people and a substitute for developing new human relationships. It's also not the same as seeing God so much in the natural world that one is no longer able to see God as being at least as strongly present in the lives of other people.

We are all like Roberto in having a deep need for other people in our lives, even if we at times are reluctant to acknowledge that need. Those of us who have lived in the same neighborhood for decades and have many long established friendships may not feel the same need to meet new people as Roberto. That need is nevertheless present, even if we do not recognize it. While we gain rich rewards from long established friendships, new relationships help us see life from different perspectives and offer us new insights. Christ may often seek to come to us and to enrich us through the introduction of new people into our lives.

If we truly think about Christ being present in each person we encounter, then we realize that there is potential significance for every new relationship in our lives. The strangers we meet can be sources of great blessings and may one day be friends who are very important to us. God also brings other new people into our lives because there are blessings that we need to share with them.

Our tendency to spend time only with those we already know limits us and keeps us from receiving all the blessings God seeks to offer us. If we routinely avoid contact with strangers and try to minimize our interactions with people we do not know, we are in fact cutting ourselves off from meaningful experiences with the presence of Christ in those persons.

Bad Things Do Happen, But. . .

Bad things do happen. Crimes are committed every minute of every hour of every day. Natural disasters occur. As people of faith, however, we must continually strive not to let excessive fear rule our lives and separate us from others. Let's look at some of the ways we've been encouraged to be more fearful than is appropriate.

In his insightful book *The Culture of Fear*, Barry Glassner raises some fascinating questions:

> *Why, as crime rate plunged throughout the 1990s,*
> *did two-thirds of Americans believe they were soaring?*
> *How did it come about that by mid-decade 62 percent*
> *of us described ourselves as 'truly desperate' about*
> *crime—almost twice as many as in the late 1980s, when*
> *crime rates were higher?* [p. xi]

Politicians, the media, and others have created a culture of fear that affects all of us. In the United States, we pour a hundred billion dollars a year into criminal justice systems, primarily for police and prisons. Yet increases in persons imprisoned and in the size of police forces do not always correlate with reductions in crime.

Consider some of the statistics shared on the page opposite the beginning of this chapter. By the figures of the U.S. Department of Justice, if current incarceration rates continue, one out of every twenty people will serve prison time in his or her life. That's an incredible percentage. And the statistics show that black males and Hispanic males are more at risk than white males.

Many of those incarcerated are not there for violent crimes. In the federal prison system, only 17% are there for violent offenses. Only a fourth of local jail inmates are normally being held for a violent crime. One can logically ask why we are keeping in prison so many persons who do not pose any physical threat to society.

According to Barry Glassner, 75% of parents surveyed fear their children being kidnapped by a stranger. The truth, however, is that most missing children have been taken by a noncustodial parent or are fleeing abusive parents. There are claims of up to 800,000 missing children a year in the United States, but only 200 to 300 abductions are conducted by a nonfamily member and result in the child being missing for a long period of time or murdered [Glassner, p. 61]. Obviously 200 to 300 instances a year is excessive, but it doesn't justify the high sense of danger which most parents feel from strangers. The sad truth is that children are in the greatest danger from their own custodial and noncustodial parents–not from strangers. But the vast majority of parents are not abusive, and the vast majority of noncustodial parents would never take a child.

Racial fears also govern much of how we live and how we respond to strangers. In the United States, those racial fears are most strongly held by white people and are directed at black people. Caryl Rivers, in *Slick Spins and Fractured Facts*, talks about the way media coverage of violent crimes emphasizes race. Through television news reporting, "night after night, black men rob, rape, loot, and pillage in the living room" [p. 161]. The same news coverage focuses far more on white victims than on black victims.

Politicians and the news media were quick to criticize the violent lyrics of rapper Tupac Shakur. The same view was not taken, however, of Johnny Cash singing "I shot a man in Reno just to watch him die." In the classic song *Sixteen Tons*, Tennessee Ernie Ford warned that those who don't step aside when he comes will die. Shakur, in fact, had many nonviolent raps and urged black men to stop killing. That did not protect Shakur himself from violence.

Paranoia about homosexuality has also swept through North America. For many of the Christian faith, there are complicated biblical and theological questions concerning homosexuality. While many persons are convinced that the overall weight of Scripture does not condemn homosexuality, others point to a relatively small number of biblical passages and maintain that homosexual behavior is always sinful. There is room for persons of good conscience to disagree on this issue. Those theological questions, however, do not constitute a basis for fear of homosexual persons or an excuse for a lack of hospitality toward homosexuals.

There is no evidence that homosexual persons are greater threats to children than heterosexual persons. There is clear evidence that the disease AIDS affects both heterosexual and homosexual persons. Homosexual persons are in fact more likely to be the objects of hate crimes by homophobic people than to themselves be the cause of violence.

Many clergy, sadly, have fanned the flames of homophobia by continual harangues on this issue. They've caused some people to fear that the United States and Canada are in danger of being taken over by a homosexual agenda and that the church itself is in danger of being taken over by homosexuals. Some churches have felt it important to develop clear statements which exclude persons of homosexual behavior, and sometimes simply homosexual orientation, from membership and involvement. Yet the reality is that homosexual persons are no different than others in wanting acceptance and in not going places where they are not welcome. Any church which encourages contempt for homosexual persons need not be concerned that homosexuals will become members.

There is considerable evidence of homosexual persons wanting to have their rights protected by the laws of society. There is likewise evidence of them wanting to be accepted and affirmed by others, just as heterosexual people want to be. There is no evidence of a homosexual agenda which threatens the well-being of the dominant heterosexual society. Our fears too often overwhelm our logic and our decency.

Fear can have many consequences beyond our own uneasiness and damaged relationships. Our fear can cause hatred, and hatred can lead to evil. When we fear persons of another race or of another sexual orientation or of a different background, that fear can turn to hatred. The forces of evil are drawn to fear and prey on it. Matthew Fox shares this counsel in *Confessions*:

> *These evil forces prey on fear. How important!*
> *So much fear runs the world, that of fundamentalism*
> *for example. Only when fear lets the evil in does*
> *evil happen. Thus, the importance of spirituality–*
> *to build the strength, the big heart (courage)–*
> *based on faith, i.e., trust, which is the opposite*
> *of fear–that combats evil successfully.* [p. 192]

In **Ephesians**, we are reminded of the reality of evil forces in the world. "For our struggle is not against enemies of blood and flesh, but against the rulers, against the authorities, against the cosmic powers of this present darkness, against the spiritual forces of evil in the heavenly places" [v.6:12]. Our fear strengthens those evil forces and closes us to the blessings God wishes to give us through other people.

The Feathered Guest

Birds frequent the Clapps' back yard because of a bird feeder, a bird bath, and a number of flowers and plants. On a summer evening, when Steve was in Ohio visiting with Fred, Steve's wife Sara, discovered an unusual feathered visitor. The bird seemed to be hiding in the cage that supported a tomato plant. The creature was brightly colored and was in size larger than a parakeet but smaller that any parrot she had seen. Sara offered food and water which the bird accepted, though it drank very little.

The bird was still there when Steve came home around midnight. They both expected it to leave in the morning, but they were wrong. They offered more food, and it proved tame enough to jump onto Sara's back, a spot from which it was not inclined to move. They didn't have a cage at hand, or they might have captured it for its protection. Its wings had been clipped, however, so it did not appear likely it was going to go over the tall fence that surrounds their yard. Flying seemed difficult enough for it, that Steve and Sara were a little surprised it had made it into their yard. Sara suggested that perhaps their St. Francis statue had drawn it.

It was a beautiful bird, but neither of them knew what kind. They called the zoo, which was not missing any birds. They called the animal control office, which didn't have any current reports of missing birds but did help them identify their guest: it was a cockatiel. They called people in the neighborhood, trying to find the bird's owner. They called the newspaper and placed an advertisement searching for the owner.

Steve felt a little stupid calling the zoo and animal control without being able to identify the breed of the bird, but people both places were kind and helpful. *The Fort Wayne Journal Gazette* and *News Sentinel* placed the advertisement without charge, which is a standard policy of those papers for FOUND pets. Neighbors phoned other neighbors to seek the bird's owner. Two people who had lost cockatiels called, but this particular bird did not belong to either of them. The bird's owner was not found, causing one to wonder if the bird was simply set free, which is not a good plight for a bird so thoroughly domesticated.

The bird's situation elicited kindness not only from Steve and Sara but also from many others. Through the efforts to help the bird, Steve and Sara had a number of very interesting interactions with other people and learned some things about birds they would not have known otherwise. The bird which appeared in their yard as a stranger became a guest and a source of blessings. That's what happens with strangers of the human variety too.

Margaret and Frank never felt comfortable around homosexual persons and felt homosexual behavior was sinful. Bill, their only child, lived on the opposite side of the country and only came home twice a year: once at the time of his birthday and once for Christmas. Margaret was afraid of flying, so she and Frank never made the cross country trip to visit Bill at his home.

Then came the Christmas that Bill came home and shared two pieces of information which were hard for Margaret and Frank to accept. First, he told them that he was homosexual. Second, he told them that he had AIDS. His physical appearance told them that he probably did not have long to live.

Margaret and Frank loved Bill dearly, but they didn't know how to respond to this news. After Christmas, Bill returned to his own home across the country, with Frank and Margaret promising that they would come visit him and meet his partner. Bill had not brought his partner home for Christmas, fearing that it would be more than his parents could handle.

But Margaret and Frank never made the trip. Their son died two months after Christmas. Their son's partner, Evan, arranged to have the body shipped back and returned himself for the funeral, which Bill had wanted to be conducted by the minister of his parents' congregation. Evan arranged to stay in a motel, and Margaret and Frank were relieved. They felt slightly guilty for not inviting Evan into their home, but their feelings were too ambivalent to extend the hospitality.

They had polite words with Evan at the funeral home and after the funeral service. They made vague promises to "keep in touch," but all three of them knew that they wouldn't be doing that.

The one consolation Margaret took was that she believed there was nothing else as awful as having a son die of AIDS that could ever happen to her. She was wrong. Only a few weeks later, her husband died in an automobile accident. Margaret was devastated. Within the space of only a few months, she had learned that her son was homosexual, had her son die, and then had her husband die.

Margaret's faith in God was deep, and that was what pulled her through the difficult days that followed. In talking with her minister, she confessed that she felt deep regret for not having visited with her son when he was so ill. She wished that she had understood more of what was happening in his life and why he was homosexual. She also wished she knew more about AIDS. But, she told her pastor, "There's nothing to be done now. I can't learn anything more about my son."

"Perhaps not," her pastor responded, "but you could learn more about someone else who is having a similar experience. There's a hospice program in town that needs volunteers to help people who are dying of AIDS and don't have family to help them."

"I could never do that," Margaret protested. "I would be far too uncomfortable. And those people wouldn't want help from someone like me."

"Those people, Margaret," her pastor counseled, "are not as different from you as you may think. Here's a phone number."

She put the phone number on the bulletin board beside her kitchen telephone. She thought about throwing it away several times over the next three weeks, but something kept stopping her.

Then she read a morning devotion with this line: "Risk stepping outside your comfort zone. God is waiting for you with great blessings just the other side of that zone." She dialed the number and attended an orientation for volunteers.

Margaret was assigned to Zack, a young man only a couple of years older than her son had been. Zack did not have long to live, but he did not want to be part of the residential hospice program. He wanted to stay in his own home. A nurse's aide helped him medically, but he needed someone to shop for groceries for him and to help with household tasks. Margaret was very uneasy about the arrangement, but Zack reminded her just enough of Bill that she kept going back to his apartment.

When she had begun to feel a little more confident around Zack and a little less afraid of visiting with him, she asked him why he wasn't receiving help from a partner or from his parents. She learned that his partner had already died of AIDS and that Zack had taken care of him. Zack cried as he told her that his parents simply could not accept his homosexuality and wanted nothing to do with him. Margaret left the apartment that day and collapsed in tears on the front seat of her car, filled with compassion for Zack and horribly afraid that Bill had felt similar rejection from herself and from Frank. She prayed to God for forgiveness for her difficulty in fully accepting her own son. As she prayed, she found her mind drawn again and again to these words: "But you can accept and love Zack."

And she did. She wanted to learn everything she could about Zack. He was open in talking to her, and she soon found herself pouring out her heart to him. She brought pictures of her husband and son. She told him about Bill's childhood, and Zack told her about his own. As they continued sharing over the next few weeks, she began to understand how much Zack had not wanted to be homosexual. To him, it did not appear a matter of choice; it was how he was programmed. Margaret had never been able to accept that view of homosexuality, not even in Bill, but she struggled to understand as Zack tearfully shared the inner battles he had experienced.

Zack died four months from the date of Margaret's first visit to his apartment, and he died holding Margaret's hand. He had no will or living trust, and he had no money left. His parents refused to have any part in the funeral, so Margaret planned it and paid for it.

The day after Zack's funeral, she made two phone calls. The first was to the hospice center to request another volunteer opportunity. The second was to Evan, to see if he would come spend Christmas in her home so they could talk together about Bill.

God is with us even in the midst of great tragedy. And strangers are often the means through which God brings healing and blessings to our lives.

Strangers and Blessings

"Do not neglect to show hospitality to strangers, for by doing that some have entertained angels without knowing it" [Hebrews 13:2]. The story of Margaret and Zack is powerful, but it is not unique. Lives are transformed on a continuing basis through interaction with strangers:

- Bob, a member of the Ku Klux Klan, experienced car trouble on a deserted stretch of highway late at night. He was at first terrified when a car with three black teenagers stopped by his. The three teens, however, were filled with goodwill and cheerfully repaired his car for him. Bob found himself genuinely enjoying the interaction with them and being impressed by their intelligence and warm sense of humor. They refused to accept money for their help, and the last words he heard were one of them saying, "Hey, God be with you, man." His life was changed.

- Betty was eighty years old and had never cared very much for young children. She had been an only child and had never married. Betty was more than a little dismayed when the house next to hers was purchased by a family with three young children. The second day after they moved into the house, her fears were confirmed when she saw two of the children walking through her flowers. She yelled at them, told them to never again come onto her property, and then phoned a fence company. The third day, the two children appeared at Betty's door with a plate of cookies, a bouquet of flowers, and profuse apologies for damaging her flowers.

The fourth day, the children's mother came and invited Betty to join them for supper. The fifth day, Betty called the fence company and told them not to come.

- Harry was a widower and lived alone. He dearly loved his adult children, but they and their families lived hundreds of miles away. He woke up one morning feeling particularly lonely and discouraged. He started to take his heart medicine and then thought, "Why bother? What am I really living for?" He walked to the 7-11 store three blocks from his house to buy a newspaper and a cup of coffee. A new clerk was working at the counter and cheerfully introduced herself to him. The store was not busy, and he found himself visiting with her for ten minutes. He told her about his children, and she said, "I'll bet they miss you as much as you miss them." Harry went back to his home and took his heart medicine.

- By the age of fourteen, Brian had been in front of a judge three times. The judge ordered him to participate as a volunteer at a soup kitchen run by a Catholic parish. Brian discovered that the soup kitchen was run by Alice who was seventy-two years old and was not about to be intimidated by someone who was fourteen. At first he feared her. Then he hated her for making him do tasks over repeatedly until he did them right and for making him apologize when he was rude. But then he found his feelings for Alice beginning to change because, in spite of his difficult behavior, she really seemed to like him. Soon Brian realized that he looked forward to going to the soup kitchen to work, and he

began to find himself talking with Alice about what was
happening in his life.

How might your life be transformed by interaction with people
you do not yet know? What impact might you have on the life of
someone else? Who are the angels you might be asked to
entertain?

Keeping Safe in Thunderstorms

- If you are outside and can hear thunder, then you are close enough to be struck by lightning. Find shelter.

- Do not take shelter in small sheds, under isolated trees, in convertibles, or near fences or poles. Seek a sturdy building.

- If you are in the woods, take shelter under the shorter trees.

- If you are outside and feel your hair stand on end or your skin tingle, squat low to the ground and place your hands on your knees with your head between them. You want to minimize contact with the ground and make yourself the smallest possible target.

- Get out of boats and avoid water.

- Avoid telephone lines and metal pipes, which can conduct electricity.

- Do not take a bath or shower.

- Turn off air conditioners. The power surge from lightning can overload the compressor.

- Unplug appliances not needed for weather information.

Based in part on information from the New York State Disaster Preparedness Commission.

Chapter Four
Prayer and Hospitality

Concept: True hospitality is only possible when our lives are grounded in prayer and intimately connected with God. Prayer can transform the fundamental way in which we view the world around us.

What happened to the cockatiel who was introduced in the last chapter? Steve and Sara Clapp finally placed it in a cage and began an unsuccessful campaign to find its owner. The cockatiel, however, had other plans.

The weather was good, and they left the caged cockatiel on a deck, thinking that it was pleasant for the bird to be in the sunlight. They also were afraid that, if they brought the cage into the house, their cats would terrorize the bird. The cage they used to house the cockatiel was one that had been used in house training their dog. The bars looked narrow enough to confine the cockatiel who initially made no serious effort to escape. The bird ate well and interacted pleasantly with Steve, Sara, and their curious dog.

But the cockatiel apparently decided he (or perhaps she) had experienced enough of their hospitality and managed to escape from the cage by some kind of unwitnessed maneuver. They searched the neighborhood and left out special cockatiel food for two days, hoping the bird would return. With crows and cats patrolling the neighborhood, they didn't feel the rather friendly bird was likely to survive a long time.

Thus Steve can't provide a satisfactory ending to the story of the cockatiel. He simply does not know what happened to the bird. In wonderful hindsight, he wishes that he had brought the cage into his study and kept the cats shut out of the room. Steve and Sara had been unsuccessful in finding the bird's owner, but their inquiries had resulted in more than one offer of a good home for the bird. Sara thinks it may have been a mistake to cage the cockatiel while searching for its owner. The bird seemed to be enjoying their yard and interacted pleasantly with them. Perhaps the bird would have continued to stay in the yard until a home had been found if they had not put it in a cage.

While hospitality usually produces blessings, not every interaction with strangers will have a happy ending. The cockatiel certainly was a blessing to Steve and Sara in various ways, and presumably the bird benefited from the food and attention received. Steve and Sara cannot help wishing that there had been a different ending to the story.

Hillary and Brad reached out to a couple their age who moved into their neighborhood. As soon as the movers had finished unloading, Hillary took a plate of cookies to their new neighbors. Amy and Ted were delighted by her welcome, and the two couples began to develop a relationship. Both households had young children who became friends.

Amy and Ted started attending the same church as Hillary

and Brad. While Hillary and Brad were aware that money seemed a little tighter for Amy and Ted than for themselves, that did not concern them; in fact, Hillary and Brad tried to find small ways that they could be of help, especially by sharing clothing their children were outgrowing.

Then they started noticing that Ted wasn't leaving for work as early in the morning as he had been, though he was gone much of the day. After a week of this new pattern, Amy confided to Hillary that Ted had been fired and was looking for a new job.

A week later, Ted approached Brad and asked for a small loan to help with groceries and their electrical bill. Amy, like Hillary, had only a part-time job because of the age of their children; and that pay didn't stretch very far. Brad was glad to help and also suggested that Ted seek an interview with Brad's employer. Over the course of the next month, Hillary and Brad loaned over a thousand dollars to Amy and Ted. When they felt that they couldn't advance more money, they referred Amy and Ted to the pastor of the church who helped them from the emergency fund the church maintained for such needs. Ted and Amy didn't have family to whom they could turn for help, and they were very grateful for what Hillary, Brad, and the church did for them.

Ted did end up getting a job with Brad's company, largely through Brad's influence. With his first paycheck, Brad started repaying the money borrowed from Hillary and Brad and said that he wanted to repay the church as well, though the pastor had made it clear that no repayment was expected.

Six weeks later, Ted was fired. Brad learned from Ted's supervisor that Ted had lacked the flexibility needed and that, when pushed to change, he had shown a strong temper, something Hillary and Brad had never encountered. Hillary and Brad were determined to remain their friends and had them over for dinner the weekend following Ted's termination.

Over the next three months, Ted had and lost another job; and the debt of Ted and Amy to Hillary and Brad increased by another thousand dollars. The pastor also advanced more money to them. Amy tearfully acknowledged to Hillary that Ted's temper was a problem from the beginning of their marriage. The first three years had been reasonably good ones, because Ted worked for a small business owned by his father. His father made allowances for his son's temper and once fired another employee who couldn't get along with Ted. Then Ted's parents were killed in an automobile accident, and Ted had not been able to keep the family business going.

Amy maintained that Ted had never been abusive to her or their children, and Hillary and Brad never saw a direct display of Ted's temper. The situation, nevertheless, felt increasingly awkward as Amy and Ted's financial situation deteriorated, and Holly and Brad felt unable to do anything further.

The problem was resolved when Ted got a job in another city. This time they moved themselves, using a rented truck. Brad, Hillary, and some others from their church helped in the move. Ted and Amy promised Hillary and Brad that they would stay in touch and would eventually repay the money they had borrowed.

They did repay about half the money, and Amy and Hillary communicated by e-mail for several weeks. Then Amy said in an e-mail that Ted had been fired again and that they weren't sure what they were going to do. The e-mails stopped coming, and there were no more payments on the money which was owed. Hillary and Brad tried to call, but the phone number was no longer in service. Then Hillary and Brad sent a letter, telling Amy and Brad to forget about the debt but to please keep in touch with them. The letter was returned by the postal system with "NO FORWARDING ADDRESS ON FILE" stamped on it.

Hillary and Brad showed genuine hospitality and compassion to Amy and Ted. Their congregation and pastor also showed compassion and a willingness to help. Hillary and Brad felt more let down by the failure of Amy and Ted to stay in contact than by the fact that the money did not get repaid. Yet they also were not sorry that they had done what they had to help these strangers who became friends.

Not Optional and Not Safe

In our first book together, we titled the first chapter: *Hospitality: Not Optional and Not Safe*. We feel that the Old and New Testaments make it clear that Christian people are to practice hospitality. It is not optional. When we fail to practice hospitality, we are closing our hearts to the blessings God wishes to share and to the presence of Christ in other people.

Perhaps the most significant New Testament admonition about hospitality comes in the parable of the Good Samaritan, which was told by Christ to answer the question "And who is my neighbor?" [Luke 10:29b]. The Samaritan "was moved with pity" [v.33] for the man who had been injured, helped him, and arranged for his continuing care by the innkeeper. Our obligations are not just to the people we already know.

But the practice of hospitality is not always safe. Someone we choose to befriend may turn out to be manipulative or dishonest. Some may be essentially honest but have such serious problems, like Ted and Amy, that our efforts do not have the result we want. We may occasionally extend hospitality toward those who will reject us. We may find that the practice of hospitality leads us into contact with persons we would otherwise have avoided.

Following the example of Christ has never been a guarantee of a problem-free existence. Reaching out, as Christ would have us do, does not free us from pain and suffering. We may see the pain and sorrow of the world more clearly than ever as we attempt to look at others as Christ would have us look.

The page opposite the beginning of this chapter has counsel for keeping safe in thunderstorms. Some parts of North America have to worry about earthquakes; some are frequented by tornadoes; coastal areas can be damaged by hurricanes. All parts of the continent endure thunderstorms.

We anticipate thunderstorms as a part of the natural world. We take precautions, but we don't stop going outside because of them. We learn what we need to do in order to be safe, and we accept occasional thunderstorms as a part of life. Likewise, we need to anticipate some problems in relationships with others, but we should not let those stop us from building new relationships.

Our own strength and our own insight, however, are not sufficient to draw us into lives of greater hospitality and compassion. The person who wants to show Christ-like hospitality and compassion must seek to develop the spiritual life so that Christ's love and strength are continually available. True hospitality is only possible for a life which is grounded in prayer and intimately connected with God. Prayer can transform the way we feel about ourselves, the confidence with which we relate to others, and the fundamental way in which we view the world around us.

This does not mean that we postpone the practice of hospitality until we have reached a certain level in the development of the spiritual life. It does mean that we seek to develop the spiritual life at the same time as we seek to practice greater hospitality. Christ continually seeks to bless us through the people around us and through our lives of prayer.

Prayer and Hospitality

According to Gallup polls and other surveys, most people in North America pray. That includes many people who are disillusioned with organized religion but who still feel a connection with God. Some people pray frequently throughout the day; some pray occasionally; and some pray primarily when faced with a particular problem or dilemma.

Both of us consider ourselves more students than teachers when it comes to prayer. There are limitations on what we or anyone else can effectively teach on this topic. In *Reaching Out*, Henri Nouwen reminds us that:

> *The paradox of prayer is that we have to learn*
> *how to pray while we can only receive it as a*
> *gift. . . . We cannot plan, organize or manipulate*
> *God; but without a careful discipline, we cannot*
> *receive him either.* [p. 87, p. 89]

Prayer, ultimately, is a gift from God. God continually seeks to deepen connection with each of us, and our efforts at prayer are always received and cherished by God. The beginning bedtime and meal prayers of a small child are just as pleasing to God as the eloquent prayers of a minister or theologian.

With considerable humility, we offer these guidelines for people who want to deepen the life of prayer, especially in relationship to the practice of hospitality:

1. Most of us need to pray with greater frequency and regularity if we are to be more fully open to God's guidance in our lives. Changing from a fearful life to a more confident life of hospitality and compassion is not an easy transition. Occasional prayer will not provide the foundation that we need for a different kind of living. We need God's help on a continuing basis, and God's guidance is most likely to come to us in small stages rather than in sweeping revelations.

In his book *In the Name of Jesus,* Nouwen writes:

> *God is a God of the present and reveals to those*
> *who are willing to listen carefully to the moment*
> *in which they live the steps they are to take toward*
> *the future.* [pp.3-4]

While we make major commitments during our lives, the living out of those commitments happens on a daily basis. Our values are most clearly revealed and our habits are most deeply defined by the decisions and actions of each new day.

Most people reading this book lead busy, perhaps almost frantic lives. Many of us do not feel that we have the time for daily devotions. Those who take that time, however, almost always find that the other activities of the day flow more smoothly.

A life of greater prayer can start in very small ways. Consider, for example:

- Starting the day with prayer.

- Saying prayer before each meal, including a silent prayer when in the presence of school or work colleagues.

- Saying a prayer each time you get behind the wheel of a car or each time you board public transportation.

- Ending the day with prayer.

The prayers can be very short, sometimes only one or two sentences. If you are not currently praying on a daily basis, simply doing one of the above options will change the way you view the world around you and will deepen your connection with God. In a few weeks time, try adding another time for daily prayer to your schedule. Don't be angry with yourself when you fail to do so; simply do better the next time.

2. Work toward a life of greater prayer, in which intimacy with God is a part of everything that you do. As you add more times of prayer to your life, you'll find yourself living more consciously of God's presence and guidance. You'll find yourself drawn more and more deeply into God's presence in the midst of your other activities. In *A Testament of Devotion*, Thomas R. Kelly describes another way of living:

> *There is a way of ordering our mental life on more than one level at once. On one level we may be thinking, discussing, seeing, calculating, meeting all the demands of external affairs. But deep within, behind the scenes, at a profounder level, we may also be in prayer and adoration, song and worship, and a gentle receptiveness to divine breathings. The secular world of today values and cultivates only the first level, assured that there is where the real business of humankind is done. . . . But in a deeply religious culture [people] know that the deep level of prayer and of divine attendance is the most important thing in the world. It is at this deep level that the real business of life is determined.* [p. 27]

Kelly also declares that, when we are immersed in the love of God, we may begin to see people differently. Some people we may have been inclined to ignore in the past begin to become more important to us. We may also find ourselves less willing to make unworthy compromises for the sake of approval by those whose values are not consistent with our understanding of God's will.

By God's grace and with a commitment to change on our own

part, we may find ourselves sharing short prayers for guidance in the midst of our daily activities:

- A prayer before making a decision at home, at work, or in another setting.

- A prayer before meeting someone for the first time.

- A prayer of thanksgiving for a new individual met by phone, by e-mail, or in person.

- A prayer for forgiveness when we have spoken in haste or in anger.

- A prayer for God's help to another person, even to those we see but do not actually know.

- A prayer for God's guidance during a meeting or conference.

- A prayer of thanksgiving in the midst of the day for those we love.

- A prayer of thanksgiving for a blessing we receive.

- A prayer for God's consolation when we are disappointed by others.

At first, we may be very conscious of those short prayers throughout the day. Over the course of time, those prayers can become as natural to us as breathing. *A Testament of Devotion* tells us that it is possible, in time, to live a life that is fully immersed in prayer and in direct connection with God.

A sense of God's presence in our lives will inevitably result in changes in the ways that we view other people. Kelly referred to this as "a tendering of the soul, toward *everything* in creation" [p.35]. As we begin to recognize the presence of Christ in each person we encounter, we will find ourselves loving others more, judging them less, and not very often feeling fearful of them.

3. As we gain confidence in the life of prayer, we can begin to risk prayers for greater openness to God's guidance. In her marvelous book *A Christian View of Hospitality–Expecting Surprises*, Michele Hershberger writes:

> *I decided to pray every morning for God to send me a hospitality opportunity, a person I could host, a person who would be Jesus to me.* [p. 13]

Such a prayer is a brave one, because God will respond. When we are truly open for new opportunities to interact with others and to do God's will, God will guide us in that process. This is the kind of prayer that has the power to transform our lives. We can pray it with confidence as we gain trust in Christ's guidance and protection of our lives.

Some Prayers for Deeper Intimacy with God and Others

The best prayers are often the prayers of our own hearts, and sometimes they consist of an opening of ourselves to God rather than any verbal expression. In the development of the spiritual life, however, the prayers which have been written by others can play an important role. Worrying too much about how to express ourselves to God can be a barrier to intimacy. The prayers others have found helpful may enable us to express our own desires and hopes. Some prayers have been found so meaningful by so many people that they have been passed down through the centuries.

In this section, we offer a few prayers which may be helpful as you seek to deepen the connection between prayer and hospitality. Some of these prayers do not deal directly with our interactions with other people but deal rather with an overall attitude of openness to God's guidance and help. That attitude inevitably leads to hospitality and away from fear.

Prayers at the Start of the Day

Rejoice in the Lord always; again I will say, Rejoice. Let your gentleness be known to everyone. The Lord is near. So do not worry about anything, but in everything by prayer and supplication with thanksgiving let your requests be made known to God. And the peace of God, which surpasses all under-standing, will guard your hearts and your minds in Christ Jesus. [Philippians 4:4-7]

My dear Lord, who hast made my soul Thy dwelling place and will never leave me, I ask Thee to rule me, govern me, enclose me, and make me one with Thee in perfect charity. Amen. [Juliana of Norwich]

I pray that, according to the riches of his glory, he may grant that you may be strengthened in your inner being with power through his Spirit, and that Christ may dwell in your hearts through faith, as you are being rooted and grounded in love. I pray that you may have the power to comprehend, with all the saints, what is the breadth and length and height and depth, and to know the love of Christ that surpasses knowledge, so that you may be filled with all the fullness of God. Now to him who by the power at work within us is able to accomplish abundantly far more than all we can ask or imagine, to him be glory in the church and in Christ Jesus to all generations, forever and ever. Amen. [Ephesians 3:16-21]

O God, Who art the unsearchable abyss of peace, the ineffable sea of love, the foundation of blessings, and the bestower of affection, Who sendest peace to those that receive it, open to us this day the sea of Thy love, and water us with the plenteous streams from the riches of Thy grace. Make us children of quietness, and heirs of peace. Enkindle in us the fire of Thy love; sow in us Thy fear; strengthen our weakness by Thy power; bind us closely to Thee and to each other in one firm bond of unity; for the sake of Jesus Christ. Amen. [Syrian Clementine Liturgy]

O God, I give you deep thanksgiving for the gift of this new day and for all the blessings which will be contained in it. Grant me a discerning heart that I may truly recognize your presence in all those with whom I come in contact this day. Help me, Lord, to be your presence to others; and enable me to receive the gift of your presence from those around me. Forgive me for my sins and for my continuing tendency toward self-centeredness. Keep me open to your guidance and help in the midst of the opportunities, problems, joys, and sorrows which this day may bring. When anger, greed, jealousy, or frustration make it hard for me to recognize your presence in others, clarify my vision and deepen my love. Amen. [Steve and Fred]

Prayers at the End of the Day

I know, O Lord, and do with all humility acknowledge myself an object altogether unworthy of Thy love; but sure I am, Thou art an object altogether worthy of mine. I am not good enough to serve Thee, but Thou hast a right to the best service I can pay. Do Thou then impart to me some of that excellence, and that shall supply my own want of worth. Help me to cease from sin according to Thy will, that I may be capable of doing Thee service according to my duty. Enable me so to guard and govern myself, so to begin and finish my course, that, when the race of life is run, I may sleep in peace, and rest in Thee. Be with me unto the end, that my sleep may be rest indeed, my rest perfect security, and that security a blessed eternity. Amen. [Augustine]

Remember, O Lord, this city wherein we dwell and every other city and country, and all the faithful who dwell in them. Remember, O Lord, all who travel by land or water, all that labour under sickness or slavery; remember them for health and safety. Remember, O Lord, those in Thy Holy Church who bring for her good fruit, are rich in good works and forget not the poor. Grant unto us all Thy mercy and loving-kindness, and grant that we may with one mouth and one heart praise and glorify Thy great and glorious name, Father, Son, and Holy Ghost, now, henceforth, and forever. Amen. [Chrysostom]

Thank you, Lord, for the many gifts you have given me. Thank you for your presence in those with whom I have shared the events of this day. Forgive me for those times when I failed to recognize your presence in others or when I was tempted to put my own desires ahead of your will. Gently guide me, Lord, as I seek to more fully desire what you desire and to more fully see others through your great love. Help me overcome the fears which separate me from others and from the best in myself. Grant me a safe night's rest, and be with me in the events of the new day. Fill me with your love, and guide me in sharing that love with others. Amen. [Steve and Fred]

Prayers in the Midst of the Day

Lord Jesus Christ, have mercy upon me. [The Jesus Prayer]

Help me, Lord, not to be weary of doing little things for your great love. Thank you for regarding not the greatness of the work, but the love with which it is performed. Amen. [Brother Lawrence]

Intensify Thy leadings and drawings in our hearts until their clarity cannot be mistaken, and incline our wills toward them. Lay on us afresh the brothering of the souls of those about us and give us the patience to persist. Kindle in us such a longing for Thee that it will illuminate and blaze through all that we do. Amen. [Thomas R. Kelly]

Prayers for God's Guidance

Gracious Holy Spirit, so much of my life seems to revolve around my interests and my welfare. I would like to live just one day in which everything I did benefited someone besides myself. Perhaps prayer for others is a starting point. Help me to do so without any need for praise or reward. In Jesus' name. Amen. [Richard J. Foster in *Prayer–Finding the Heart's True Home*, p. 201]

O Lord, our Saviour, who hast warned us that thou wilt require much of those to whom much is given; grant that we whose lot is cast in so goodly a heritage may strive together the more abundantly to extend to others what we so richly enjoy; and as we have entered into the labours of other people, so to labour that in their turn others may enter into ours, to the fulfillment of Thy holy will; through Jesus Christ our Lord. Amen. [Augustine]

Eternal source of love and forgiveness, direct us to have the spiritual insight to know that those who try to harm us are in need of our forgiveness and mercy. May we realize that the way to destroy a personal enemy is by overcoming evil with good, by praying for those who persecute us. [George Fox, founder of the Society of Friends]

My Father, if it is possible, let this cup pass from me; yet not what I want but what you want. [Matthew 26:39–the prayer of our Lord at Gethsemane]

Lord, I am conscious of living so much of my life governed by fear. I fear failure, I fear rejection by others, I fear being taken advantage of, I fear sickness, I fear lost opportunities, I fear change, I fear death. Surround me with your great love, and help me put aside my fears. Let me have no fears except those which are appropriate for protection and safety and the doing of your will. Deepen in me a spirit of compassion and hospitality toward others. Grant me this day an opportunity to practice hospitality to another, to be your presence to someone in need. And make me ready, Lord, to receive the blessings you are ready to give me through others. Amen. [Steve and Fred]

More Thoughts on Children and Guns

- Children should be taught that if they encounter a gun, they should SALT:
    - Immediately **S**TOP whatever they are doing.
    - **A**VOID touching the gun.
    - **L**EAVE the area at once.
    - **T**ALK to an adult about the gun.

- Hiding a gun is not enough to make children safe. Children can go through all the drawers and cabinets in a house. Even very young children climb on furniture, ladders, or stepping stools to explore high shelves. The best child-proofing methods are the same ones that keep unauthorized adults from gun access OR not having a gun at all.

- Many locking cases for guns have three wheels with numbers on the locking mechanism. It takes an average of only ten minutes to open those locks by systematically trying every combination.

- Children need to be told about the danger of playing with guns. They also need to know the difference between violence in the media and real-life violence.

- Guns and ammunition should be stored separately and locked. Unloaded firearms should also be provided with a gun lock, gun alarm, or another device to prevent tampering and to make the gun inoperable. Gun storage keys should never be kept in the same location as other keys.

- Do you really need a gun?

Chapter Five
Hospitality and the Family

> **Concept:** Hospitality has the power to transform how we view our spouses, parents, children, and the others who constitute family. We need to develop appreciation for the changing nature of family in our time.

"What just amazes me," Carolyn said to her pastor, "is that our daughter went from 125 pounds to 84 pounds before we recognized that something was wrong. Jill had always been so healthy. She ate right. She took part in sports. She did well in school. We just didn't worry about her as much as we did about her older sister or her younger brother.

"She picked up the pace of her physical fitness work, and we were a little concerned about her overdoing, but we didn't want to pour cold water on her enthusiasm. What should really have tipped us off a lot earlier was that she became so picky about what and how much she would eat. It started becoming hard to cook anything that she would eat that the rest of the family would like. When she suggested that she just start fixing her own meals, I was actually a little relieved. I wondered in the back of my mind if she had some kind of eating disorder, but it felt to me like that was something that would happen to someone else's child, not to ours.

"We saw that she had gotten very thin, and sometimes that worried us. But most of this happened during the fall and the winter, so we weren't seeing her wearing sleeveless blouses or shorts and didn't realize just how thin she had become. We'd try talking to her about her looking thin, but she got very defensive. We thought that, after all, she was sixteen years old, so there was a limit on how much we should be trying to control her.

"Then one day in the spring, she came downstairs wearing shorts and a tank top to go for a run. I looked at her, and her arms and legs just looked like sticks to me. I told her that we had to go into the bathroom and use the scales to see how much she weighed. She started crying, and I had to physically drag her to the scales. She got on them, and she was at 84 pounds, including the weight of her clothes and running shoes.

"We went straight to our family doctor's office. I don't know if I will ever be able to forgive myself for not recognizing what was happening sooner. I guess I just didn't want to deal with it until it was so clear there was no choice at all. And then I wonder what my husband and I did that caused her to develop the eating disorder. Where did we go wrong?"

Keith did not know Carolyn, but he certainly could identify with not having faced a problem as early as he should have. Keith came home from work on a Friday evening to find his wife's closet empty and a note taped to the beer in the refrigerator:

> *Keith, I'm sorry to do it this way, but you just don't*
> *hear me when I try talking to you. Being married to*
> *you feels like being in prison. I know you mean well*
> *and think you're protecting me, but what you're doing*

is controlling me. I earn as much money as you, but
you make all the financial decisions. If you feel like
sex, we have to have it whether I feel like it or not.
You decide where we go for Thanksgiving and Christmas.
My family always has to take second place. It's gone on
for nine years, and I can't handle it any longer. You
pushed it over the edge two nights ago when you said
that it was time for us to have a child. I've been wanting
to do that for two years, but you wouldn't have it. Now
that you're ready, you expect me to rearrange my life
and my career so we can do it. Keith, I'm sorry, but
I realized that I don't want you to be the father of a
child of mine. I love you, but I can't live with you.

Becky

The practice of hospitality certainly involves reaching out to strangers and to persons we do not know well, but it also impacts how we relate to those who are the closest to us. True hospitality means that we recognize the presence of Christ in those with whom we share our lives. And hospitality has nothing to do with ownership or control. Hospitality means recognizing that the other persons in our lives are guests and that those relationships are gifts from God to be cherished. For most of us, the practice of hospitality has some important implications for our relationships with family and close friends.

Hospitality and Our Children

Carolyn suffered from deep guilt for not having more quickly recognized the seriousness of her daughter's eating disorder. With perfect hindsight, she can recognize the signs that should have motivated action from herself or her husband. Parents all over North America, however, have had similar experiences. It's easy to fall into the trap of ignoring or rationalizing away events linked to problems that are painful to face. Hospitality is not a cure for Carolyn's dilemma, but a life focused on hospitality does have some implications for parenting.

1. Hospitality recognizes that children are gifts from God, not properties to rule over. That in no way means that children should not be disciplined and taught to behave. Recognizing our children as gifts from God carries with it the responsibility to raise them with the values, beliefs, and habits that are appropriate for all the sons and daughters of God.

The focus of our decision-making in raising our children, however, should be on what is best for them rather than on what is best for ourselves. In our fast-paced society with what seem like ever-increasing demands in the workplace, it's easy for us to begin seeing our children as an inconvenience. Tired from the work and stress of the day, we can all too easily be tempted to take the easy way when dealing with our children. Many parents come home from work needing to relax and unwind, and they understandably do not want "one more thing" to deal with or handle.

The needs and problems of our children, however, are not just "one more thing" to handle or one more problem to solve. They are gifts from God, entrusted to our care. There is nothing that those of us who are parents do which is of any greater importance than taking the time to make the right decisions concerning our children. That can at times mean confronting them about concerns over drugs, weight loss, or sex.

Bill visited with a group in his church about the pace of life in his family. He said, "What really got me was when our son asked if we would help him buy a motorcycle. The first thing I thought of was, 'If he gets a cycle, then we won't have to drive him places anymore.' I felt this relief wash over me, and I started to say, 'Sure, we'll help you get one.' Then I realized that I was thinking of my convenience and my wife's convenience. I wasn't thinking about whether or not a motorcycle was a good thing for him to own at his age or whether or not it was good for us to help him buy one.

"I also wasn't thinking about all the conversations that we have with him when we drive him to practices and meetings and games. I know all that has to end sometime, but is this the time that it should? Maybe we have one more valuable year of being his transportation. Anyway, the decision shouldn't be about what is easiest for us."

2. Seeing our children as guests reminds us that we are not responsible for everything that they do. Our children are far more than extensions of us. They are not going to handle every situation in the way that we wish they would. No matter how hard we try, we are not going to be able to protect them from every problem which life brings. Henri Nouwen, in *Reaching Out*, provides this perspective:

> *The awareness that children are guests can be a liberating awareness because many parents suffer from deep guilt feelings toward their children, thinking that they are responsible for everything their sons or daughters do.* [p. 57]

Those are words of comfort for parents like Carolyn who find themselves obsessed with the question: "Where did we go wrong?" There's not always a clear answer to that question. Eating disorders, drugs, alcohol, early sexual activity, school problems, social problems, financial hardship, depression, suicide, and other difficulties that afflict our children usually have multiple causes.

Parents can take on themselves too much responsibility for what happens to their children and for what their children do. Hospitality recognizes that children are guests in our lives, that they have their own identity and values, and that we cannot and should not attempt to control everything that they do. This reality becomes especially true as our children grow and mature. Recognizing that we want them to mature into the people God has created them to be should free us to increasingly let go of our efforts to control as they move through adolescence.

"The problem for most of us," Carol, a child psychologist, said to a parenting class at her church, "is that we don't do enough to influence the behavior of our children when they are small and then that we try to regain control when they become teenagers. That never works. If you're going to use the word control, then the time to exercise control is when children are young. When we try to increase our control over their behavior after they hit the teen years, we are going against the normal developmental tasks of that age, which are focused on their taking increasing responsibility for their own decisions and breaking free of our control."

3. Practicing hospitality with our children means doing our best and then trusting the result to God, who is the

parent of us all. Susan, a single parent, talked to her mother about her feelings on parenting. "I felt like such a failure when Angie was having so much trouble as a child. The divorce was hard on Angie and David, but David didn't seem as badly affected at the time. David was thirteen, and Angie was seven when we separated. David seemed to just move ahead as the perfect child, trying to take care of Angie and of me.

"Angie had such serious problems. She couldn't sleep at night. She pulled her hair and picked at her skin during the day. She didn't deal well at all with living with me during the week and with her father on the weekends. As I look back, I realize that I neglected David a lot of the time because Angie was so demanding. How could I ignore problems that severe?

"But Angie came through those years and has turned out fine. She has such a healthy self-confidence as a college student that it's hard to believe she had so many problems as a child. David is the one I feel badly about now. He's doing all right with his life, but he's told me a couple of times how much he hated his sister those years right after the divorce and how angry he was with his father and with me for giving all the attention to Angie. He felt neglected, and he was right. He just always seemed to be doing well, and that's what we wanted to believe."

"But what else could you have done?" her mother asked. "You certainly couldn't ignore Angie's problems. You only had so many hours in the day, and you had to work and earn a living. Your ex-husband was in the same spot. You made the best decisions you could at the time. Sure, you can look back now and see that more should have been done for David. But where would you have found the time to do it? David may carry some anger, and you need to let him talk about it. David, however, has turned into a fine young adult, and he's having a good life. Both of your children turned out well."

"Perhaps I wouldn't feel this way," Susan acknowledged, "if we'd never gotten the divorce. I've always assumed that Angie's problems came about because of the divorce."

"Maybe they did. But there could have been a different set of problems if you'd stayed married to each other as angry as the two of you had become as husband and wife. What you have to recognize is that you did the best job you knew how to do. It wasn't perfect, but God doesn't expect perfection of us. You need to cut yourself some slack and be thankful that your children both turned out so well."

Susan's dilemma is one which many parents experience as we live in a time when two out of three children in the United States will spend at least part of their childhood in a single parent home. The nature of family life has changed. We may not feel good about that in many ways, but it is a fact of life. Raising a child is difficult for a husband and wife together, and it is even more challenging for a single parent.

The truth is that, as parents, we don't do everything right. The marriage decisions that we made before having children weren't always the right ones, and there are consequences that flow from that as well. What we are called to do is our best. We must trust the results to God.

4. Hospitality does mean taking seriously our responsibility for the children God has entrusted to our care.

The page opposite the beginning of this chapter provides *More Thoughts on Children and Guns*. It is very difficult to have a gun in the house and to be absolutely certain that children will not get access to it. A police officer kept her service revolver in a case which had three wheels with numbers on the locking mechanism. She had the code set to **7, 7, 7** because she thought that would make it easy for her to access the gun in an emergency. She felt confident that the locking mechanism was adequate to protect her children.

While clearing the table one evening with her husband, they heard their two children giggling loudly from the master bedroom. They weren't alarmed, but they did wonder what the children had gotten into. They walked into the bedroom and discovered their five-year old son aiming the service revolver at their three-year old daughter. The children were both giggling as the big brother said, "Raise your hands, or I'll shoot!" The gun was loaded.

Children are incredibly creative—and at times downright crafty. Their son proudly told them that it had taken him only a few tries to get into the gun case. He knew that the security code on their household burglar alarm system was **3, 3, 3** so he figured the numbers on the gun case would also be a single number repeated.

Police officers have guns. Clearly that particular officer needed a new solution for storing the gun while at home. But how many of the rest of us really need to have weapons? For most of us, the probability of needing a weapon in self-defense is much smaller than the probability of the weapon being used to injure or kill someone we love.

Hospitality means not being governed by our fears in the community–or in our own homes. We want to protect our children, but that at times may mean protecting them from our own fears.

The fact that children are guests in our homes should free us from unhealthy guilt over all that they do; but far from absolving us from responsibility for protecting them, it increases the magnitude of that responsibility. These are the children of God, entrusted to us. We do not protect well when fear dominates our thinking.

And fear can affect our thinking in more ways than having firearms too readily accessible. Many of our children and grand-children lead lives which are frantic as they participate in every possible school and community activity. It's no wonder that people like Bill are relieved when it's possible for children to start transporting themselves to activities and events.

But there is a possibility that our lives have become too frantic, that both we and our children are attempting to do too many different things. In our desire to see that our children have every experience possible, we may be overloading them and ourselves. We fear depriving our children of important opportunities or making ourselves appear "different" from others by not participating in the same activities, but the frantic pace which results may be depriving our children of other needful experiences. The quality of family life inevitably suffers when people are pulled too frequently in too many different directions.

Those of us who are active in churches need to be careful that the multitude of church activities we participate in do not further pull our families in a conflicting directions. Most of the time, however, the church comes in second place to the demands of school activities, athletic events, and other opportunities. Missing a swimming or hockey or music practice can put a child off the team; missing a youth group meeting does not carry similar consequences.

What do we really want to have happen in the lives of our children? How busy is too busy? How can meaningful family time be protected? What priorities do we teach our children by the decisions we make with them? These are all serious questions as we think about our responsibility to the guests in our homes.

Spouses and Significant Others

In a meeting with parents of teenagers, Steve asked the group what they felt their children needed to be taught to prepare them for dating experiences and marriage. One parent said, "By all means, teach them to put their marriage partner first, not last. My husband and I are continually giving each other the leftovers. We put our work first and then some of our other obligations. We share with each other the time and emotional energy that remains when everything else has been done. That's no way to nurture a relationship with the person you love more than anyone else in the world."

It sure isn't. The trap she described, though, is one which snares many couples of all ages. We are busy. We are often under stress. There are work demands and community demands and parenting demands and (for many of those reading this book) church demands. It's easy to have little time, energy, or patience left for one's spouse or the person one hopes will become a spouse. What does hospitality say about the way we interact with our most important partners in life?

1. Hospitality means that we see the spouse as a cherished gift of God, not as a person to be controlled. Control issues were at the root of the problems Keith and Becky had, as described in the beginning of this chapter. Keith in fact did not recognize just how controlling he had become of Becky and of their relationship. Unable to successfully communicate with him about it, she finally left.

Our expectations of marriage are sometimes unrealistic. It's not at all unusual for a person to get married with the anticipation that his or her partner will change over the course of the relationship in certain desirable ways. Life continually involves change, of course, but it's very unrealistic to expect that another person can be molded into the image we desire. Our efforts to change each other in intimate relationships become efforts to control, and those efforts are resented even when they are successful.

It's easy to convince ourselves that our desires to change a spouse are rooted in wanting what is best for the spouse and for our relationship. That may indeed be our intention. But the result is rarely positive. People do not want to be shaped by someone else. Hospitality teaches us to cherish rather than to control and to work openly on mutual change rather than inflicting our will on the other person.

2. Hospitality means sharing equally in decisions about money, sex, children, and other vital areas of life together.

Recognizing the other person as a gift from God, with whom we have the opportunity to share a lifetime, means more than an absence of control. It means working together positively to shape the kind of life together that will be most meaningful.

Couples who believe in hospitality, who recognize the presence of Christ in each other, are not going to be concerned about which person earns the most money. They are going to be concerned about making mutual decisions concerning the use of the material resources that they have.

Becky and Keith had fallen into the trap of Keith making all the decisions concerning their sexual relationship. If he was in the mood, something happened. If he was not in the mood, nothing happened. Becky had to feel like an object that was owned rather than a person who was cherished.

Decisions about children also need to be made together, recognizing Christ's presence in each other and in the children God has given. When children are young, one parent, who is able to spend more time at home, may appropriately carry a larger share of the nurturing function. That does not mean that the other parent should be excluded from major decisions affecting the lives of their children, and it certainly does not exclude the other parent from the responsibility of being involved in the lives of their children.

In all these areas and others, viewing one's spouse as a person to cherish means a continual desire to share in major decisions. That's part of the joy of life together.

3. Hospitality means treating one's partner BETTER

than anyone else, not worse. The decision to marry another person and the decision to have children are the two most important relationship decisions which we can make. Those are the relationships which should receive our greatest energy, our greatest commitment, and our greatest patience. One's husband or wife should not receive our emotional leftovers.

That doesn't mean it's always easy to put the other person first, especially during times of high stress at work. Obviously the best intentioned and most sincere of us will make some mistakes in this area, and it's important to readily extend understanding and forgiveness to each other. But if one recognizes that a spouse is continually receiving or giving emotional leftovers, then it's time for a careful look at where time and emotional energy are going.

4. And those who are reading these words and are single should remember that being single does not mean being incomplete. As wonderful as marriage can be, that isn't the route for everyone. Not all people are called to be married, and not all people will thrive in a marriage environment.

Parents and Grandparents

We can all celebrate the fact that people are living longer than ever, and that trend appears likely to continue. Changes in lifestyle and advances in medical technology have made it possible for many of us to live longer, healthier, more vibrant lives than were possible in some earlier generations.

With these improvements in life quality and life expectancy, however, have come some increased concerns about how to relate to elderly parents and grandparents. Adult children, already under pressure from work, from home, and from community responsibility, may find it difficult to relate as positively as they want to their own parents and grandparents. The matter is further complicated by the fact that some people live hundreds or even thousands of miles from their parents or grandparents.

Again, we need to think about these relationships from the perspective of hospitality. Our parents and grandparents are truly gifts from God, without whose love we would not ourselves exist. Certainly there are not any perfect parent-child relationships, and our relationships with our parents and grandparents can sometimes be clouded by unresolved issues. That reality, however, should not be permitted to blind us to the presence of Christ in them and to the very special relationship which their lives have to our lives.

Fran attended a spiritual life workshop. During the course of that workshop, she identified one of her chief spiritual burdens as her failure to do as much as she should for her parents, who lived five hundred miles away. She had a brother who lived ten miles from them, and it had become easy to depend on the brother for offering help to them when needed. As she prayed in a silent time in the workshop, Fran realized that her parents did not particularly need her help, they needed her. And she still needed them. The lack of connection with them filled her with guilt and even affected her relationship with her husband and with her own children. She at times found herself resenting having moved so far from her parents because of her husband's employment and not being able to visit them more often because of the vacation plans made as a family.

She resolved that it was time to make some changes. She wrote down four resolutions at the workshop:

1. To start calling her parents once a week, every week. If her husband and children were home and could be part of the conversation, fine. But she was no longer going to avoid making the call because others were not there to share in it.

2. To involve her husband and children in more advance planning for holidays and vacation time, so that the need to see her parents wasn't continually squeezed out by last minute decisions.

3. To make at least one trip a year by herself to visit with her parents in addition to whatever traveling she did there with her husband and children.

4. To start writing a letter once a week to her parents. They loved getting written communications, and it would only take her a few minutes to do it.

As she started acting on those resolutions, she felt a significant burden lifting from her shoulders and felt her life being enriched by the deepened connection with her parents. They were overjoyed by the change. And the fact that Fran started viewing contact with her parents as important began to cause her husband and children to view it as important as well. They learned to cherish her parents, and their own lives were enriched.

The Home as a Place of Hospitality

As Steve grew up, the dining room table in his family's home was the site of many significant activities. The dining room itself was located in the center of the house. One passed through the dining room to get from the front of the house to the kitchen and family area or to get from the back of the house to the living room.

The oak table was circular and had first belonged to Steve's great-grandparents. It had been in his mother's home throughout her childhood and then had been a gift from her parents. When Steve (an only child), his mother, and his father ate at home, they sat at that table. They shared prayer before each meal, and they sometimes had devotions at the table after supper.

The table was also where his mother, a teacher, graded papers during the evening and where Steve often did his homework. Though his father more often used a desk for his work at home, he would occasionally join Steve and his mother at the table. His father, who liked practical jokes, would sometimes deliberately cover the papers of Steve or his wife with his own work and not reveal what he had done until they had searched in vain for their materials.

When there were family decisions to be made, they sat together at that table. Steve's decisions on church membership, college choice, and graduate school selection were all made at that table. His parents decided there when to buy and sell their small businesses (a restaurant, a tavern, and a movie theater) and when to retire. Steve remembers meaningful conversations with his parents when people they knew died or experienced great tragedy in their lives. He also remembers times when his father, who was a township supervisor and thus responsible for financial assistance to many people, sat at that table to talk with those who were experiencing difficulty in their lives.

They often entertained, and it was easy for a couple of other persons to join them at the table. His father sometimes invited transients who came to him for financial assistance to join the family for a meal, and Steve's life was enriched through the discussions with those persons. For larger groups, there were additional leaves which could be inserted in the table, so that it could comfortably accommodate at least ten people.

Steve's parents are deceased, and the table now sits in an office Steve maintains in a local church. He continues to work at that table occasionally, and it's also the setting for various meetings. Each Sunday a young adult class in the church gathers around the table to talk about the Bible. And Steve feels certain that his parents would be pleased at the kind of conversations that happen at that table.

There is a sacred quality to that dining room table because of the ways in which it has been used over the years. Steve can still sit at the table and feel a strong sense of connection to his parents and to God.

Many of our homes have places or objects which become symbols of our faith, which are made sacred by the manner in which they are used. For some it may be a dining room table; for others a sofa; for some couples the bedroom is a place of both physical and spiritual intimacy; for others a grill, coffee pot, popcorn popper, or refrigerator door. Some families focus on objects like a Bible, a cross, a candle, or a family cup which take on special significance. Think about such places or objects in your own home. What would they be? How can you use such objects or places as part of the ritual of your home life?

The home is one of the primary settings in our lives for the practice of hospitality. It is the place where we show hospitality not only to those who live together as part of the family but also to those who visit us. If we want to broaden our hospitality, the home setting is a wonderful place for doing so.

The Scriptures remind us of the power which comes from sharing food. **Isaiah 25:6** proclaims:

> *On this mountain, the LORD of hosts will make for all*
> *peoples*
> *a feast of rich food, a feast of well-aged wines,*
> *of rich food filled with marrow, of well-aged wines*
> *strained clear.*

The Lord's Supper or Eucharist has roots in the traditional Sabbath evening meal that was common in Jewish homes and in the Passover meal which was celebrated annually. The ordinary substances of bread and wine take on special meaning. **Luke 14:13-14** reminds us that Jesus wants us to invite a broad spectrum of guests to the meals we serve:

> *But when you give a banquet, invite the poor,*
> *the crippled, the lame, and the blind. And you*
> *will be blessed, because they cannot repay you,*
> *for you will be repaid at the resurrection of the*
> *righteous.*

Think about these questions:

- How fragmented has your home life become? Could you benefit from a greater effort to eat one meal a day together as a family? Would a weekly devotion at mealtime help the quality of spiritual life in your home?

- How welcome do the friends of your children feel in your home? How could you help them feel more welcome? If you have no children at home, are there children in your neighborhood who would enjoy your hospitality?

- How frequently do you invite other family and friends to share in meals and to visit in your home?

- Have you considered inviting people who are new to your neighborhood or church to come share in meals with you?

- Have you thought about the possibility of sharing your home with an exchange student? With a foster child? With someone recovering from a drug or alcohol problem who needs a place to live? Is it possible that God is calling you to a ministry of such hospitality?

Remember that hospitality does not depend on the affluence reflected in our homes or on the amount of time spent preparing a meal. While we may be self-conscious concerning the quality of our home furnishings or the cleanliness of our rooms, those who visit us form their opinions based on the warmth of our welcome rather than on the physical characteristics of the house. In the busy times in which we are living, an elaborate home-cooked meal, while certainly appreciated, may not always be realistic. We can show hospitality through the sharing of pizza, soup and sandwiches, or carry-in food. Again, it is the warmth of the welcome we show others that determines their response to our hospitality. We should not let too little time and too much pressure keep us from the blessings that come to us as we use the home as a base for hospitality to others.

Children and the Internet

- The Internet is a fantastic resource for people of all ages and offers exciting opportunities for children. Just as you wouldn't let your children be near a busy street without supervision or rules, you need to help them be safe and wise in their use of the Internet.

- Explore the Internet with your child. Learn more about the interests of your child and provide guidance. Go to sites especially developed for children.

- The best tool your child has for being safe on the Internet is his or her mind! Teach children about the presence of pornography, hate literature, and exploitation on the Internet and help them understand why you don't want them exposed to it.

- Use a commercial Internet Service Provider which offers parental controls that can block many kinds of offensive information.

- Continue to monitor your children when they are online. If they start to become uneasy or defensive when you enter the room or visit, that could be a sign they are doing something of which you would not approve.

- Warn them about giving out their name, address, password, phone, or school to people they don't know. Remind them never to agree to meet face-to-face with someone they've met online. They should always talk with you about such requests.

Chapter Six
Nurturing Hospitality

> **Concept:** How hospitality can help us reclaim a sense of community in the neighborhoods where we live, in the workplace, with the people with whom we do business, and with some persons we may encounter only once.

During the summer that we were completing this book, Fred, his wife Joice, and three members of their family made a trip by car from Ohio to Alaska. As they crossed into Canada, customs officials asked Fred, who was driving their vehicle, if they had any firearms, mace, or pepper spray. Fred replied that they did not. Then he was asked more specifically about rifles, shot guns, or handguns. When he responded negatively to those questions, he was asked if they had any weapons at home. Fred said that they did not.

They were asked to pull aside. Then they were asked again about weapons and about their destination. When the women in the group went inside the customs station to use the restroom, they were approached by a female officer who asked, "Don't the men have any firearms? It would be better to tell us." They responded by saying that there were no firearms and that, as a part of their church tradition, they did not believe in violence and chose not to own weapons.

Their vehicle and luggage were searched, and of course no weapons were found. As they worked at repacking the vehicle, Fred asked one of the Canadian officers why there was so much concern about weapons and why they had been searched. He was told, "It's very unusual for us to encounter people from the United States who don't have weapons. They may not have brought them along, but they almost always have them at home. When you said that you had no weapons at home, that made us think you could be lying, so we decided to search your vehicle. You people in the U.S. have such fear that you arm yourselves. That's not allowed in Canada and frightens us."

The Absence of Hospitality

Of course it's impossible for us to know all the thinking that went into the searching of Fred's vehicle by the customs officials. Perhaps people heading for Alaska are considered more likely to be going hunting; perhaps the number and age of the people in the vehicle was a factor. In any event, it is clear that those of us in the United States have cause for concern if we are appearing as fearful to people in other countries as the Canadian authorities indicated to Fred.

The interaction with the customs officials posed an interesting issue of hospitality for Fred and his family. How does a person show hospitality to those who are questioning your integrity and making your life difficult by searching your vehicle? Fred and his family chose to respond to all the inquiries with honesty and with courtesy, even when the tone of officials was not particularly courteous toward them.

When they had been cleared of carrying any weapons, it was possible for Fred to ask for further explanation of what had happened and to make a stronger witness to his own beliefs about avoiding both violence and weapons which can be used for violence.

The lack of hospitality that affects most of our lives truly stands at epidemic proportions. Those of us who fly commercially are familiar with the questions about who packed our bags, with the occasional search of checked baggage, and with the metal detector screening process. Authorities feel sufficiently fearful of the possibility of terrorist activity to treat all airplane passengers as though they were potential criminals; and as a public, we have accepted enough of that fear not to complain about the process. The authors of this book aren't in favor of abandoning airport security, but that security process does contribute to the fearful manner in which we live.

In the process of talking with others about this book, we had several persons talk to us about the lack of hospitality that they had experienced in hospitals. It seems particularly ironic to experience this short-coming in an institution whose name is found in the word hospitality!

People who go to the hospital often are fearful—patients are fearful of what procedures may be inflicted on them and of what those procedures may reveal; friends and family are fearful for the welfare of those they go to visit. Those who manage and work in hospitals are presumably not fearful of the patients, friends, and families who come; but hospital employees are often working under huge amounts of stress and are perhaps governed in part by fear of not doing their jobs right. The result, unfortunately, is sometimes an atmosphere that is not conducive to the healing that hospitals exist to provide. Those of us who work in hospitals or visit them frequently on a professional basis, such as clergy, may start to take the atmosphere for granted. Think about these situations:

- A woman spent six hours in the surgical waiting area, waiting to be informed what was happening to her husband, who had required immediate surgery because of a tragic automobile accident. Her persistent requests to the staff member on duty were met with the firm reassurance that she would be contacted when something was known. As it turned out, however, her husband had been out of surgery for three hours, had been in the recovery room without her, and had been taken to a hospital room. She had received no notification from the physicians, nurses, or reception staff. She finally got his room number by calling hospital information from a pay phone in the lobby. Her husband had been very concerned about why she was not with him but had been unable to get anyone to check on her location.

- A man who was 83 years old was informed by a cardiac surgeon, on the basis of an arteriogram, that he needed to have immediate bypass surgery. The man's overall health was not good, and both he and his wife felt that they needed another opinion before agreeing to such a major surgery. The surgeon was offended by what he took as a lack of confidence on the part of the patient and his wife. In order to leave the hospital and to get another opinion, the patient had to check out "against medical advice." He and his wife felt badly treated not only by the surgeon but also by the nursing staff and the administrative staff of the hospital, all of whom were angry over their not immediately accepting the recommendation. They went to a university-connected medical center for a second opinion. It was the unanimous opinion of three specialists there that he should not have bypass surgery. His body was already forming collaterals around the most damaged coronary artery, and he was sufficiently weak from other health complications that he was not a good candidate for the surgery. The man just celebrated his 88th birthday and feels much better than he did at 83.

And of course there are numerous other examples that could be shared. Many people reading this book have had the experience of being made to feel that their insurance coverage and financial health were of greater concern to a hospital upon admission than their physical health.

Hospitals and medical staff who make a concerted effort to be sensitive to the needs of patients and to help patients feel less fearful can create a very different atmosphere. It is often a matter of focus. Those hospitals which see the needs of staff members and the institution as the primary purpose for their existence rarely reflect positive hospitality. Those which are focused on the needs of patients and their families extend a courtesy, a helpfulness, indeed a hospitality which help the healing process and lower the fears of those who enter their doors.

Lack of hospitality, of course, isn't always related to fear. Sometimes the lack of hospitality which we experience is simply based on discourtesy, on being in too big a hurry, or on failing to think about the consequences of our actions. Some of us, who show decent hospitality under ordinary circumstances, display a different personality when we get behind the wheel of an automobile. How often have you seen someone:

- Complaining about other people all driving too slowly and getting in the way?

- Complaining about other people all driving too fast and recklessly?

- Honking the horn when disgusted that someone else is not reacting more quickly to a traffic condition, even though no one is in danger?

- Swearing about someone else's driving?

- Needlessly cutting off someone else?

- Speeding up to make it difficult for another person to merge in front?

- Speeding up to make it hard for someone to pass?

Or is it possible that you yourself may have fallen into some of those behavioral traps?

The page opposite the beginning of this chapter shares some guidelines concerning children and the Internet. E-mail and the Internet bring new opportunities to display both courtesy and rudeness to others. The Internet is in many ways an impersonal medium; we often do not know the persons with whom we interact in Chat Rooms or from whom we read messages on Internet bulletin boards or discussion groups. Because e-mail can be written so quickly, many people fall into the trap of making angry responses to things which irritate them, often sharing statements that they would never make over the telephone or place in a traditional letter.

Some readers of this book will remember the case of Karla Faye Tucker, who was convicted of murder and in February of 1998 became the first woman in many years to be executed. Because of a religious conversion while imprisoned which seemed to truly transform her life, many people, including some within the prison system itself, attempted to get her life spared by the courts or by the governor of Texas (the state in which she was convicted and executed). For two weeks, Steve followed a very hot debate through an Internet bulletin board. Steve was concerned about the fact that the opinions ran about two to one in favor of her execution. Coming from a peace tradition, Steve was not comfortable with capital punishment and especially not in this situation.

When he posted a couple of thoughts of his own about the debate, he discovered that not all the responses from others to him went to the bulletin board–some came directly to him by e-mail. Much of that e-mail reflected very strong emotions. For example:

- "She deserves to die and good riddance to her."

- "Rip her arms and legs off, and then chop her into hamburger to feed the other losers on death row."

- "You are a pathetic son of a b---- to have taken her side."

- "You dirty son of a b----. You've probably never lost someone you loved, or you'd be in favor of the murder of everyone like her."

The anonymity of the Internet certainly lowers the inhibitions of people. It's very doubtful that those same people would have written letters to Steve with the same language and even more doubtful that they would have used it in a face-to-face conversation with him.

But those nasty responses do not have Steve soured on the process of online discussion. He sent this response to everyone who referred to him in terms that reflected negatively on his mother:

> *I wonder if any of us think through the way that we use words in the anonymous environment of the Internet and of e-mail to people we don't know. You are probably a good person, but you used some language that is a problem to me. My mother died last year, and it upsets me to have people try to insult me by using language which reflects negatively on her memory. I sincerely hope that was a result of strong emotion and not really a reflection of your character.*

Steve sent those words to fifteen people, and three of them wrote back expressing their regret and thanking him for making them aware of the impact of their words on others.

The practice of hospitality is not helped by the reality that we live not only in a fearful time but also in an annoying time. Everyone reading this book has no doubt had to deal with the annoyance of marketing phone calls during the evening. In a single evening, one of the authors of this book received by phone:

- A "special, limited" offer on siding for their home.

- Two credit card offers.

- One disability insurance offer.

- A college alumni fund-raising call.

- A local charitable institution fund-raising call.

- An offer of a "free" weekend in a hotel in exchange for visiting a new time-share in Florida.

- A call offering a lower mortgage rate from a company which had incorrect information on both name and address.

- Two calls which had no one on the line–almost certainly because they had been automatically dialed and then no sales agent was free when the phone was answered.

It's enough to make you get caller ID. And it's enough to make you feel very uncharitable toward those who call. Telemarketing folks have also come up with an interesting choice of words when the person they want is not home: "There's no message; this is just a courtesy call." A courtesy call that interrupts the evening meal? We don't think so! Certainly those calls reflect an absence of hospitality on the part of those who are phoning, but decisions about how to respond to those calls challenge our understanding of hospitality.

Reclaiming Hospitality

We do not have to be victims of our own fears or of the fears of others. We may not be able to change the attitudes of customs officials, airport security guards, insensitive hospital staff, or telemarketers; but we can modify our own attitudes and behaviors. It's possible for us to reclaim meaningful hospitality in a wide range of relationships with other people, including persons we may not know and may never see again. In this section we offer some specific strategies which may be helpful to you.

Behind the Wheel

1. When getting behind the wheel to drive, consider saying this prayer:

> *Keep me safe as I drive, Lord. Help me to be alert
> and careful. Protect me from what I cannot control.
> Help me, Lord, to be aware of your presence in the
> other drivers and pedestrians I encounter, especially
> in those whose actions may be irritating to me. Grant
> me patience, kindness, and hospitality toward all I
> encounter. Amen.*

2. Remember that very few of us by excessive hurrying or taking chances make any significant difference in how

long it takes to reach our destinations. Hurrying across a railroad track, speeding through a yellow light, or cutting off someone else, however, can cause an accident, which might permanently keep you from your destination. If you are concerned about being somewhere on time, try leaving a few minutes earlier than usual. That single action will likely help more than all the hurrying behind the wheel of the car that one is tempted to do.

When you get stuck waiting for a train or delayed at a traffic signal, say a short prayer thanking God for the gift of the ability to drive, thanking God for the other people around you, and asking God to grant you patience. Remember that it is very unlikely that a few seconds or even a few minutes lost are going to have that great an impact on your day–unless you convince yourself that they will.

3. The fact that someone else drives like a jerk doesn't mean that you should worsen the situation by also driving like a jerk. Many of us have a reflexive response to negative behavior by others. We respond in kind without thinking about it, but that action in fact makes the environment even less hospitable. Driving an automobile that weighs one-and-a-half or two tons at speeds of thirty, fifty, or seventy miles an hour is not the best time to get into a disagreement with someone else. Don't cut off someone who has cut you off. Don't pull over to keep someone who annoys you from passing. Don't speed up to make it difficult for someone to get in front of you.

4. Take the initiative to show hospitality to other drivers and to pedestrians. For example:

- Pull back and create room to make it easier for someone to merge in front of you.

- When two lanes narrow to one, leave room between your car and the car in front sufficient to let others pull in front of you.

- When it's safe to do so in terms of other traffic, grant the right of way to pedestrians, even if they don't have it coming–especially when it's a rainy day or the pedestrian has limited mobility.

- Use your horn only to avoid accidents, not to express your irritation. If you encounter, for example, an elderly person who is driving hesitantly, be courteous and helpful if possible rather than blaring your horn and raising his or her anxiety.

- Extend special courtesy toward those riding motor-cycles or bicycles. They are more exposed than persons in cars and more vulnerable in accidents.

Remember that the other person is likely not that different than your own mother, father, spouse, child, grandparent, or grandchild. Respond as you would want people to respond to those you love.

5. When someone else extends courtesy to you, respond with a wave and a smile if possible. If someone makes it easy for you to merge or grants you the right of way, reward them with a wave and a smile. Let that person know you appreciate the courtesy. Positive responses reinforce hospitality on the road and make the day more pleasant for everyone.

In the Neighborhood

1. If you don't know your closest neighbors, change that! Look for opportunities to introduce yourself to those who live around you. Don't be a pest and don't pry into their lives, but do seek opportunities to extend friendship. If you live in a large apartment complex in a major city, try smiling at people and saying "Good morning!" They may think you are strange at first, but most people in time will begin to respond in the same way.

2. Be alert for opportunities to show kindness to those who live near you. If someone's car won't start and you have jumper cables, help out! If someone's garbage can has fallen into the street, pick it up. If you live in a winter climate, try shoveling the walk of a neighbor on an occasional basis. If your neighbor is elderly or has physical limitations, consider shoveling it all the time. If you learn that a neighbor has suffered a death in the family or has a loved one in the hospital, share your concern. Consider taking a baked dish to that neighbor's house as an expression of your sympathy. Bake cookies and take them to your neighbors at Christmas. Have a small open house with refreshments for your neighbors.

3. Pray for opportunities to become better acquainted with those who live near you. If you sincerely pray to God for help in getting better acquainted with those who live near you, those opportunities are likely to come. God honors such prayers, and the act of praying will likely increase your sensitivity to those opportunities.

4. Remember that you don't have to become "best friends" with all your neighbors in order to benefit from knowing them. In the time in which we live, it certainly is true that our closest friendships are often with people from work, from community organizations, or from church. It may well be that you aren't going to form deep friendships with those whose primary tie to you is geographical proximity. But it is not socially or spiritually healthy to be completely disconnected from those who live nearby and whom you will see on at least an occasional basis. When you know your neighbors:

- You contribute to an overall environment of hospitality and good will which benefits everyone.

- Your neighbors are more likely to notice if there is a fire or a break-in at your home and to seek help. People who know each other pay more attention.

- If you have children, neighbors who know you will take a greater interest in the safety of your children.

- If you need help with car trouble, a plumbing emergency, or another household difficulty, there may well be a neighbor who can help you.

- You will find opportunities to be Christ's presence to those around you, and you will experience that presence from others.

The Workplace

1. Get to know the people with whom you interact through your work. This counsel may seem obvious, but millions of people in North America fail to do it! Increasing numbers of us work in large companies or organizations and interact with a significant number of people. Even those of us who are self-employed have contact with clients, vendors, and subcontractors. It's easy to become accustomed to not remembering the names of everyone we encounter and to not bother getting to know anything about people that isn't directly relevant to the business at hand.

Certainly many of us work in high pressure settings where time is at a premium. Lengthy visits with others can be inappropriate and irritating under such circumstances. That doesn't mean, however, that we shouldn't try to learn the names of those with whom we interact or endeavor, when appropriate, to learn more about them. Take advantage of opportunities which present themselves:

- If you've been encountering the same person in the same department or area for weeks or months or years and don't know that person's name, introduce yourself, say you're sorry you don't know that person's name, and share appreciation for the response. Perhaps you've been talking to the same person at the counter at a printer's office without knowing that person's name. Make an introduction. The other person will welcome it.

- If someone has an interesting poster or picture hanging in his or her workspace, comment on it or ask a question about it.

- If people have pictures of their children, other family members, friends, or pets, ask about them.

- Although such things may seem trite, it is not inappropriate to ask if someone had a good weekend or had a good vacation or. . . .

2. When a coworker proves difficult or uncooperative, consider the possibility that the problem may not be related to you at all. When a coworker seems more difficult or resentful than usual, it's easy for us to jump to the conclusion that we must have done something wrong or at least something that is irritating to the other person. That's not always the case. Caring about others means being willing to be straight forward when necessary. You may want to say: "You seem upset about this project. Have I done something to make your work difficult?" OR "You seem more distressed than usual today. Is there anything I can help with?"

3. When you know that a coworker is going through a difficult time, gently express your concern. If a coworker has a family member who is ill or who has recently died, take a moment to stop by that person's workspace or make a phone call to express your concern. You don't have to initiate a lengthy conversation to make a difference. Simply say: "I was very sorry to learn that your father died. You'll be in my thoughts and prayers." OR "I just learned that your husband has been in the hospital. I just wanted you to know that I am concerned and will be thinking about you. Let me know if there is anything I can do to help." Be open to further conversation if the other person wants to talk.

Perhaps you have a coworker who failed to receive an anticipated promotion or who actually received a demotion. You may or may not know all the circumstances surrounding the decision. Usually, however, one can say something like: "I'm sorry that you didn't get the promotion. That must be very disappointing." OR "I'm sorry that you didn't get the promotion. I really enjoy working with you and value your contributions to the company." [Of course these may not be the best responses if you are the one who denied the promotion!]

4. When a coworker receives a promotion, an honor, or other special recognition, share your congratulations. We don't always think about sharing good wishes with others when good things happen to them. Many of us suffer from a little jealousy when something good happens to another person. But regardless of the circumstances, it's a good idea to congratulate others for the recognition they receive. Sharing our good wishes can help deepen relationships and can also help communication when things aren't so good.

5. When you need to talk with a coworker about a problem, do so in the most positive and least judgmental way possible. That's true whether the person is your supervisor, an employee at the same level as yourself, a person you supervise, or a person in another department or with another firm. Be straight forward in identifying problems, but try to approach the issue as you would want another person to do with you. Remember that we all make mistakes, and none of us want to lose the respect of others because we've done something wrong. People find it easiest to correct mistakes and to change their approach to problems when difficult situations are presented to them in as positive a manner as possible.

6. Don't contribute to fear in the workplace. Some organizations seem to run on fear. The board fears the stockholders; the president fears the board, the vice presidents fear the president, and on down the line the fear continues to run. Fearful atmospheres don't tend to produce high creativity or longevity of employment. You may not be able to change the entire culture of your organization, but you can make a difference in your relationships with those with whom you most closely work. Avoid threatening people and putting people down. Treat others with respect, and encourage them to do the same in their interactions. Model a positive, caring, straight forward style.

7. Don't be a part of gossip or discrimination in the workplace (or anywhere else for that matter). It's not unusual in many work settings to hear statements like:

- "Did you hear how badly Ed got chewed out by the president? He won't be around here much longer."

- "I saw Mary looking pretty down in the mouth yesterday. Do you suppose she lost the Schmidt account? We'll all be in trouble if she did."

- "Did you know that Jim was in the hospital again last week? The way he looks, I just wonder if he has AIDS."

- "I know we've got all those equal employment opportunity laws to obey, but I don't think Pete fits in well here at all. There's just too much cultural difference."

- "Did you hear about Betty filing a sexual harassment complaint against her boss? I think she's been leading him on, trying to get a raise or a promotion, and she probably got just what she deserved."

No good purpose is served by those kinds of statements. Such opinions are often based on insufficient information and the human tendency to traffic in gossip. People can be deeply hurt by that kind of gossip, because the more a statement is repeated, the more it is taken to be true. Even if statements like those just shared are true, spreading the information generally does nothing but hurt the persons who are involved.

A person who wants to practice true hospitality, who wants to recognize the presence of Christ in others, avoids saying things which may not be true, which can be hurtful, and which are not beneficial to the organization or the people involved.

8. Share compliments and positive messages when you have opportunity. You can make someone's day with just a few positive words, and you can contribute to an improved atmosphere in your organization. Try saying things like these:

- "Thanks for getting this job done for me so fast. I really feel under pressure on this project, and you've just made my life a lot easier."

- "By the way, I'm going to drop a note to the president and tell him what a great job you did on the presentation yesterday."

- "This report is excellent. Thanks so much for your work on it. I'm going to share it with several people."

- "I just learned that Amy and Brad got the Meyers account for us. Their supervisor told me that they worked every evening and every weekend for a month to do it. That's going to make a big difference for our company. I'm going to thank them personally the next time I see them. You might want to say something to them too."

Dealing with Telephone Solicitations

1. Do your best to get OFF telephone solicitation lists (unless you actually like receiving these calls). Use services that put out lists of people who do not wish to be called. When you receive an unwanted solicitation call, tell the person who calls politely but firmly, "I make it a policy not to respond to telephone solicitations of any kind. It would be better for your company and better for me if you removed my name from your list."

Remember that when you order something in response to a telephone solicitation, you are practically guaranteeing that the same company will call you again and probably that your name and phone number will be sold to other companies as "an active telephone purchaser." If you really don't want to be bothered by telephone solicitations, then truly make it a policy not to order.

2. Remember that God does love the people who make telephone solicitations (even though we suspect God might prefer that they made their living in another way). Most telephone solicitation jobs do not pay well, and the persons working in those positions have often had a difficult life. Many of them would like to be earning their living in another way. Our being rude or irritable with them doesn't keep them from calling; it simply makes the whole experience worse for them and for us. Stay polite, but be firm in declining and in asking to be removed from their solicitation lists.

3. Make a distinction between solicitation calls for sales from companies and solicitation calls for donations from organizations with which you are connected. The student calling from the college or university from which you graduated or the neighbor calling on behalf of United Way should not get the same response as the person wanting to put aluminum siding on your brick house. While declining all sales solicitation calls is a wise move, you may want to remain open to some charitable calls. Remember, however, that some charitable organizations will sell your name to others. If you don't want your name shared, you may wish to say: "I'm happy to give you a donation, but I want to make it clear that I do not want my name given to any other organization."

E-mail and the Internet

1. Never say anything in an e-mail that you would not say in a face-to-face conversation or over the telephone. Rude is rude. Discourteous is discourteous. Insensitive is insensitive–in e-mail or any other medium. Reflecting anger in an e-mail message is commonly known as "flaming" in Internet circles, and people always resent it. Like an angry printed letter, an angry electronic letter can continue to hang around for months and years and may be used against you at a future time. While delaying a response in order to cool off may clutter your electronic mailbox or computer file folders, it will help you avoid the series of electronic correspondence or personal conversations required to make peace later. Even if you don't know someone, remember that strangers over the Internet are the children of God just like strangers in your neighborhood or anywhere else.

2. Recognize that while they should not, people will sometimes say things in e-mail that they won't in printed mail. The process of producing printed mail takes longer and gives more time for thought. When someone sends you a flaming piece of e-mail, don't take offense too quickly and don't escalate the conflict by responding in the same way. That person may self-correct if given time.

3. If you have a computer or are considering one, remember that e-mail can be a powerful medium for staying in contact with people about whom you care. It's great to look in your electronic mail box and see that your parent, child, spouse, grandparent, brother, or sister has sent you e-mail. Many parents find it a very economical and convenient way to stay in touch with sons and daughters who are in college. Friends, whether in the same city or across the country or the world, often choose e-mail for the convenience and economy of the medium.

E-mail blends some of the best characteristics of a letter delivered through the mail and a phone call without some of the problems. A letter received through the mail lets the recipient read it at a convenient time, and e-mail does the same. You don't have to respond the second it comes as you do with a phone call. On the other hand, e-mail is much faster than a letter sent through the mail. When the computers and servers that transmit the e-mail are all working smoothly, e-mail communication can jump across the country or around the world at about the same speed as a phone call. The cost of sending e-mail is normally built into whatever small monthly fee you pay for connection to the Internet. That makes e-mail less expensive than a letter through the mail service and much less expensive than a phone call (unless you start to count the cost of the computer, the modem, and the software!).

4. While you certainly want to urge your children to be cautious about building relationships on the Internet, be aware that common interests discovered through this medium can be very rewarding for adults. One of the neatest things about the Internet is that there are so many people who are willing to help others and who are very generous with their time and knowledge. Questions posted to Internet bulletin boards or shared with electronic mail groups can bring you a tremendous amount of helpful information. While you may spend some time personally responding to inquiries in an electronic mail group to which you belong, you need to balance that expenditure of time with the benefit of ideas others share with you through that electronic group or in response to your bulletin board inquiries. You have many opportunities to share hospitality with others through this electronic medium, and you can be the positive recipient of the hospitality of others.

Business and Community Contacts

1. Treat waiters, waitresses, cashiers, tellers, and others courteously, recognizing that they embody the presence of our Lord. It's easy not to think much about our interactions with the people who serve us in stores, banks, restaurants, and other commercial settings. The personnel in these positions often change rapidly, and it is not realistic to think that we will build significant relationships with many of these persons. We'll only see some of them a single time.

We don't need to have a significant discussion each time we interact with a person while transacting a small amount of business; but we can use those opportunities to display friendliness, warmth, and good humor. Doing so can make a difference. Here's an example of a friend named Ruth's interactions as she spent a Friday afternoon running errands:

- When she got a quick lunch at McDonald's, she noticed that the clerk had obviously spent a long time painting elaborate designs on her fingernails. Ruth's first thought was "this person has nothing better to do with her time than paint her nails. What a waste." Then Ruth stopped herself and considered the possibility that the clerk had few things that made her feel good about herself. Ruth said to her, "The design on your nails is very intriguing. Did it take a lot of work to do that?" The clerk beamed with appreciation and told Ruth that she and her sister spent one evening a week doing each other's nails. Ruth brought pleasure to the woman and also learned that the elaborately decorated nails were linked to a family activity.

- There was a long line at the drive-through at the bank. As she sat in the line, Ruth remembered that it was the first day of the month, when many people receive their payroll or pension payments. She reflected to herself that a lot of those people needed direct deposit and an ATM card. Then she recognized that she was wanting to transfer money among some accounts and get bills of a particular denomination for graduation gifts. Others in the line could have similar needs. When Ruth's turn came, the teller greeted her over the intercom system. Ruth said back to her, "It looks like you're having a very busy day. I hope it's a good one for you." The teller responded, with added warmth in her voice, "The first of the month is always a challenge. I hope you didn't have to wait in line long." And even though Ruth had waited in line what seemed like a long time, both she and the teller felt better because of the warm exchange.

- At the Post Office, Ruth wanted to get self-stick stamps with the pink rose design. The clerk who waited on her said, "I don't have those. You can have flags or fruit, no roses." There were several other postal clerks, and Ruth wondered if one of them might have roses. She was tempted to be demanding, but then decided to use a different approach. With a smile on her face and warmth in her voice, Ruth said, "I know you have to feel swamped with all the people coming in here, but my husband and I really like using the rose design on our envelopes. Is there any possibility that another clerk might have some and that you could get them from that person?" The clerk smiled back, asked another clerk for the stamps, and then sold them to

Ruth. Ruth thanked both the clerks, who wished her a good day.

- At a superstore offering a wide variety of products, Ruth had difficulty finding the kind of light bulbs she needed and asked a clerk for help. The clerk immediately stopped stocking shelves and took Ruth to another section of light bulbs. Ruth thanked the clerk for her help and asked her how she liked working in the store. The clerk thanked Ruth for her interest and told her that it was a good place to work for a second income but that the pay wasn't enough to support a family. They shared a few additional words, and Ruth said a silent prayer for the clerk and her family as she went on with her shopping.

- Ruth stopped by the dry cleaner on her way home. She had been going to the same place for five years and was on a first name basis with the two clerks who worked there. Sylvia, the clerk who waited on Ruth this time, seemed visibly distressed. Ruth said to her, "You seem upset today, Sylvia. Is anything wrong?" And Sylvia responded by sharing a few of the problems she was having with her 14-year-old son who had a court appearance to make the following Monday. The store started to fill with customers so further conversation was going to be awkward, but Ruth invited Sylvia to call her at home that evening if she wanted to talk more. Sylvia did call her that night, initially just to thank Ruth for her concern, but she then proceeded to share more of her situation. Because Sylvia did not have a church home, Ruth suggested

that she consider calling the youth pastor at Ruth's
church because of that pastor's experience working
with troubled young people.

Ruth improved the quality of her own day and the quality of the
day for several others by the way in which she interacted as she
conducted her business. The most significant discussion, of
course, was with Sylvia. That discussion would not have been
likely if Ruth had not built a good relationship over the years.

**2. Develop a healthy interest in others, learn to ask
questions, and listen.** Many of Ruth's positive interactions
came because she was genuinely interested in the people with
whom she did business. She asked one person about her nails;
she asked another person what it was like to work in the store;
and she asked Sylvia if anything was wrong. She received a
response each time, and she listened with genuine interest.
People are hungry for positive connection with others. When we
develop an interest in the people around us and ask the right
questions, we'll learn a great deal and find our lives enriched as a
result.

**3. Say prayers for the persons with whom you interact,
even when you do not know their names.** Ruth said a silent
prayer for the clerk in the superstore, and she also prayed for
Sylvia. Ruth has also prayed more than once for patience before
going into her Post Office branch because of the negative attitudes
she has found there. At the end of each day, Ruth has the habit
of praying for each person she has encountered and seeking God's
help and direction for the new day.

4. Learn to look for and expect the best in others rather than the worst. When we experience service which is repeatedly indifferent or poor, our sense of expectation gets pulled down. It's easy to reach a point at which we do not expect to be treated well by others and as a result do not seek to treat them well. We can't change the attitudes which other people have, but we can change our own. That can be the starting point in creating a more civil, hospitable society.

Simple resolutions to be "friendlier" won't result in deep change in our habits or in the attitudes of others. What's needed is a sincere desire to recognize the presence of Christ in the lives of the people with whom we do business and to respond to them appropriately.

From a business perspective, there's nothing "weak" about this approach. When we expect the best from others, we truly want to find it. While being critical of people doesn't help them, clearly asking for what we want does. There's nothing inhospitable about saying things like:

- "I'm sorry, but this fish isn't well enough done for me. I would appreciate your having this cooked a little more thoroughly."

- "I know that you want to do the right thing. I thought this shirt would be the right size for my brother, but I was wrong. I need for you to accept it as a return."

- "I still have the same problem with my car's heating system that I did when I brought it to you for service last week. This problem is apparently a difficult one to fix. As you're working to repair it, I'd appreciate your keeping in mind that I've already paid a substantial amount. I'm hoping not to have another bill today unless there are other parts that are needed."

In each instance just shared, the speaker is firm about the need for service but is also respectful of the other person and does not immediately assume bad intentions on the part of the other person.

Practice Hospitality Wherever Possible

Fred is always positively impressed when he visits the office of his financial planner. The greeting is consistently warm, and the receptionist immediately asks if Fred would like coffee. Coffee, tea, cream, sugar, cups, and spoons are always available, making it clear that guests are expected at this place of business. Certainly one can take the view that "it's good for business to have refreshments," and that's no doubt true. Fred would still be going to the financial planner, however, even if no coffee were served. The fact that it is served increases the sense of welcome and makes the business transaction more pleasant.

Most of us should think about the opportunities we have to deepen our hospitality to those around us: to clients, coworkers, neighbors, friends, and family. Where can we add hospitality without slowing down a busy day? Where should we make a conscious effort to slow the pace of the day for a few minutes? Could you increase the level of hospitality in your life by:

- Having a dish of candy on your desk to share with

coworkers and clients?

- Offering a cup of hot chocolate to the mail delivery person on a cold winter day?

- Asking the neighbor who is collecting signatures on a petition for a neighborhood improvement to share with you in a soft drink or a cup of coffee?

- Inviting a person you would like to know better to have breakfast or lunch with you?

- Inviting a person who seems to spend too much time alone to share a meal in your home?

Sharing the Faith

Both of us have written and taught about ways to share the faith with others and to invite others to participate in the life of the church. That's not our primary focus in this book, though the concluding chapter does deal with hospitality within the faith community. The relationships we build through the practice of hospitality can provide a basis for us to visit with others about the faith, about what God means in our lives. Sometimes we fail to recognize the opportunities for such discussions when they come.

Henri Nouwen, in *Reaching Out*, suggests that unhealthy practices of evangelism in our society may have blocked our own willingness to witness to what is most important in our lives:

As a reaction to a very aggressive, manipulative and often degrading type of evangelization, we sometimes have become hesitant to make our own religious convictions known, thereby losing our sense of witness. [p. 70]

Ruth would not have felt comfortable handing an evangelism tract to the clerk at McDonald's or at the Post Office. On the other hand, she was certainly willing to visit about faith issues with Sylvia on the telephone because that was directly relevant to Sylvia's concerns.

When we focus our lives on recognizing the presence of Christ in others, then we will have opportunities to talk, without manipulation, about the role that faith plays in our lives. We do not have to manipulate in order for those openings to come; God will bring them to us if we are open to receiving them.

To Avoid Being a Crime Victim

- Keep a list of your credit card numbers and the phone numbers to report their theft readily accessible.

- Never let someone have both your social security number and your credit card number. That makes it very easy for someone to get additional information about you and to steal your identity. If a clerk in a hotel or store asks to see a photo-ID to go with your credit card, show them your license, but cover up the social security number when you do so.

- If you put your purse or packages in the trunk of your car, move the car before you continue shopping. Thieves watch for people putting items in their trunks and then going back into a shopping center.

- Don't carry unnecessary cash. With bank machines available all over North America and Europe, you don't need large amounts of cash when traveling.

- Don't share your credit card number with someone over the phone unless YOU initiated the phone call.

- Check your credit card statements for unauthorized charges.

- Lights and a dog continue to be good ways to discourage residential burglaries. Illuminated entries and lights around the house make it harder to force entry and make the home appear occupied. Use lights on timers when you are gone. And–burglars don't like dogs.

Chapter Seven
Hospitality and the Hurting

> **Concept:** We need to discover what hospitality can mean for the poor, for race relations, for those struggling with drug and alcohol problems, for criminals and crime victims, and for others in our society who are hurting.

In *Angela's Ashes*, Frank McCourt describes the hospitality frequently shown by his mother and by others who were horribly poor. When food was at a premium, a woman in a store gave Frank's mother an onion for their sick child. A butcher sold Frank's family a pig's head for Christmas and then gave them some sausage for their Christmas breakfast.

Even though their own financial situation was so bleak that the gifts of an onion and of sausage were significant, Frank's mother always found a way to respond to others in need:

> *You never know when you might come home and find*
> *Mam sitting by the fire chatting with a woman and a child,*
> *strangers. Always a woman and child. Mam finds them*
> *wandering the streets and if they ask, Could you spare*
> *a few pennies, miss? her heart breaks. She never has*
> *money so she invites them home for tea and a bit of friend*

> *bread and if it's a bad night she'll let them sleep by the*
> *fire on a pile of rags in the corner. The bread she*
> *gives them always means less for us and if we complain*
> *she says there are always people worse off and we can*
> *surely spare a little from what we have.* [p. 273]

When Frank McCourt was older and began delivering tele-grams, he discovered that those to whom he made the deliveries often begged for assistance. His supervisors told him firmly that he must never do anything but deliver the telegram. Yet he found himself bringing telegram money orders to people who were starving and who were physically unable to do anything with the money order. They would beg Frank to get the money order cashed for them and to buy them some groceries. If he got on his bicycle and left, he would be leaving them with a money order that was useless. Thus he found himself disobeying his employers in order to help people who were starving.

While we may not be exposed to physical needs that seem as extreme as those described eloquently by McCourt, we live in a world filled with hurting people. If we take seriously the presence of Christ in others, then we have a responsibility to reach out to those persons. Although none of us individually can solve the pressing social problems of our time, each of us can make a contribution. Frank's mother, even in her times of deepest poverty, found a way to respond to persons in need; and Frank himself learned that rules were not as important as compassion.

Partly because of the fear of our time, many of us live in isolation from people with certain kinds of needs. Most of us live in neighborhoods populated by people of about our same income level and often our same ethnic background. Some of us have elaborate security systems to keep others away. If we are middle class, upper middle class, or wealthy, we may have relatively little exposure to persons who live in deep poverty or who have different ethnic backgrounds. Many of us do not have a close relationship with a person who has a serious disability.

Called to Reach Out

No matter where we live, there are of course persons with significant needs who live close to us. Even the most affluent neighborhoods have young people who are alienated from their families, single parents, persons struggling with drug and alcohol problems, and elderly persons who spend too much time alone. We need to develop a greater sensitivity to the needs of the persons with whom we are in contact on a regular basis. Much of this book, especially the preceding chapter, has talked about cultivating a greater openness to others and a greater willingness to respond to the needs of those around us.

At the same time, we need to recognize that there are persons with significant needs with whom we may not come in much contact. Most of us are not going to deliver telegrams to a person who lives in poverty and thus are not going to have the opportunity to respond which Frank McCourt did.

At a conference of Christian leaders, Steve Clapp asked 300 persons how many of them had a person of a different race as one of their four or five closest friends. Only 22 hands went up. Should we be surprised that there are so many tensions between blacks and whites or among other races when our friendship circles are not more diverse?

Most of us need to stretch our comfort zones if we are going to make a difference on some of the pressing social problems and justice issues of our time. Those problems should not be viewed as belonging exclusively to government agencies or social service organizations. If all persons are our brothers and sisters in Christ, then we need to be reaching out to those who are in need, even when they do not live in our neighborhoods. In *Reaching Out,* Henri Nouwen reminds us that:

> *From the point of view of a Christian spirituality,*
> *it is important to stress that every human being is*
> *called upon to be a healer.* [p. 65]

When most of us who claim identity as Christians let our fears and the demands of our lives keep us from being involved with persons who are different from ourselves, we contribute to a society which is far from hospitable for vast numbers of persons. We also fail to receive the blessings God waits to give us when we begin to seek interaction with those who are different from us.

Hospitality and the Justice System

Perhaps no single social issue in the United States embodies our corporate fears as much as the problem of crime and the equally large problem of the criminal justice systems which are to combat crime. None of us wants to be a victim of crime! A partial list of strategies for protection are given on the page opposite the beginning of this chapter. Most of us can readily add other cautions to that list.

As discussed earlier in this book, politicians and the media have had much to gain by making us acutely aware of the dangers posed to us by crime. Certainly the problem of violent crime is greater in the United States than it is, for example, in Canada. We all want to feel safe, and it's easy for us to ignore the facts about crime and about criminal justice systems. Consider some of the things that have happened as a result.

Juvenile Crime

In the 1990s almost every state in the U.S. passed laws to transfer more young people to adult courts. A study funded by the Walter S. Johnson Foundation in partnership with a large coalition including the National Crime Prevention Council found that those strategies do not work. For example:

- Youth offenders transferred to adult court re-offend more often and with more serious offenses than those who stay in the juvenile system.

- Youth in adult institutions are eight times more likely to commit suicide, five times more likely to be sexually assaulted, and fifty percent more likely to be attacked with a weapon than youth in juvenile institutions.

- The majority of youth transferred to adult courts spend months waiting on trial, at a cost to taxpayers of around $200 a day.

- But youth in juvenile institutions also have problems and have relatively high rates of being arrested again. An approach called Functional Family Therapy which works with youth and their families in their homes has reduced repeated offenses by 25% to 80%. It costs much less than incarceration in an adult or a juvenile facility.

You can find out more about juvenile justice issues in an excellent report titled *Less Hype, More Help* which is available online at www.aypf.org or through the American Youth Policy Forum at the address given in the *Resources* section of this book.

Problems in Jails and Prisons

Dr. Chris Schriner, a Unitarian pastor in California, reminded his congregation in a sermon of some of the consequences of our lack of concern about what happens to those convicted of crimes:

> *Our society has never provided adequate oversight of jails and prisons. Voters don't clamor for independent watchdogs who protect prisoner's rights. In fact some people hope that prisoners will have unpleasant experiences so they won't want to go back to jail. But few of us know just how badly prisoners are treated, and we may not have thought about how repeated abuse leads to anger and depression, making convicts less likely to be positive members of society when they are released.*

The Los Angeles Times, in the summer of 1998, had a series of articles on the use of force by prison guards: "The guards always gave the same paradoxical reason for resorting to deadly force. They were trying to stop fights from turning deadly. In all but a few cases [in which guards had shot prisoners to death] internal reports show, the inmates did not carry weapons or cause so much as a swollen lip while brawling."

The same series talks about violence against inmates arriving at one California prison. When a new bus pulled in, "dozens of guards snapped into drill position and performed a half-hour of football-like warmups and cheers. Wearing black gloves and tape over their name tags, the officers grabbed shackled inmates one-by-one and ran them through a gauntlet of fists, batons, and combat boots. One inmate was thrown through a window, another rammed into a wall." The same article talks about a prison at Corcoran where "problem inmates were purposely locked into a cell and subjected to repeated rapes by an inmate enforcer." That leads one to ask who the real criminals are: Those who have been sentenced? Or those who run the prisons where they are sent?

Severe Sentences

California, like many other parts of the United States, passed a "three strikes" law (three felonies and you go to jail for at least twenty years before parole eligibility). The first person sentenced under that law in Orange County was Joyce Demyers. She was a drug addict who had been arrested for robbery and burglary. Her third strike came in a sting in which she helped carry out a cocaine purchase between a drug dealer and a plainclothes policeman. Her cut of the deal was $5.00. Her sentence was 25 years to life. If she serves the minimum amount of the sentence and stays physically healthy, she will cost the state of California at least $420,000. Dr. Schriner suggested that for that sum of money, she could have a personal supervisor who spent time with her each day. That would seem absurd, but spending half a million dollars to keep her locked up also seems absurd.

While California has been singled out in some of these examples, similar problems exist all over the United States. We have been convinced that severe sentences would result in our streets and our neighborhoods being safer, and we have not thought about the consequences of those sentences.

Our Brothers and Sisters

We have in fact not thought about the persons who commit crimes as being our brothers and sisters in Christ. Most of us have been comfortable thinking of criminals as persons who are fundamentally different than the rest of us. With that in mind, we feel safest separating those persons from the rest of society. In *The Gulag Archipelago,* Alexander Solzhenitsyn, writing about his experiences while incarcerated by the former Soviet Union, reminds us:

> *Gradually it was disclosed to me that the line*
> *separating good and evil passes not through*
> *states, nor between classes, nor between parties*
> *either–but right through every human heart–*
> *through all human hearts.*

The prophet **Jeremiah** reminds us of the same reality: "The heart is deceitful above all things, and desperately wicked: who can know it?" [Jeremiah 17:9, KJV]. It is not possible to neatly separate the "good" people from the "bad" people, because the line between good and bad runs through each of our hearts. If we wanted to purge all evil from society, we would each have to tear out a pieces of ourselves.

What would it mean for us to take seriously the presence of Christ in each person? What would that mean in terms of our relationships with the victims of crime, the police, and persons convicted of crimes? A full answer to the question is a topic for another book, but here are some thoughts from the perspective of hospitality:

1. Reaching out to young people, before they are in serious trouble with the law, is likely the best single strategy to make our society safer. Church youth programs; Boys and Girls Clubs; scouting; Big Brothers, Big Sisters; and other community organizations have the potential to make a tremendous difference. Almost all of these organizations are continually seeking volunteers. There are creative court programs in some parts of North America which need volunteers to take a special interest in young people just starting to get into trouble. Could God be calling you to show hospitality to a young person through one of these programs? Certainly financial support and prayers for these efforts are important, but direct involvement offers many blessings to young people and to adults who help.

2. We need to show a true spirit of hospitality toward those persons who are the victims of crime. People who have been robbed, assaulted, stalked, embezzled, raped, or otherwise damaged through the conduct of other people often, under-standably, find it difficult to trust others and difficult not to be filled with bitterness for what happened to them. Our willingness to listen, our efforts to understand, and our demonstrations of kindness and acceptance can make a difference for those who have been victims.

3. City and county law enforcement officers are on the front lines of crime prevention, and they need our affirmation and our encouragement. They are the visible presence in most of our communities which can help lower crime and can help all of us feel safer. Their jobs are difficult, and their work is often not appreciated. There are serious problems of racial profiling and abuse of power by law enforcement officers, but the abuse of authority by some should not be permitted to reflect badly on all. People who care about justice need to build relationships with persons in law enforcement. When people spend forty hours a week or longer working heavily with persons who do not obey the law, it's easy to lose perspective. The active friendship of ordinary people lets law enforcement personnel know they are appreciated and helps them keep perspective.

4. We need to show hospitality to persons who have been convicted of crimes and to their families. If we keep in mind the reality that these persons are our brothers and sisters in Christ, then we can reach out with concern and compassion. When people we know or family members of people we know are charged with crimes, we can be a caring, supportive, nonjudgmental presence in their lives. People who are incarcerated need visitors, letters, and prayers. Their family members are likewise in need of friendship and help.

5. We should seek to be informed about criminal justice issues, to put less faith in the rhetoric of politicians, and to work for genuine reform. When justice systems fail to work and perpetuate problems rather than bring healing, those systems need to be changed. Again, a spirit of hospitality means recognizing the presence of Christ in victims of crime, in those charged with crimes, in law enforcement personnel, and (even) in politicians. Those of us who believe firmly in that presence have the ability to be advocates for changes which create a healthier society.

Too Many Issues

We've devoted about eight pages of this book to discussion of issues within the criminal justice system. Obviously a full book could be devoted to examining those problems from the perspective of hospitality. We chose to focus on criminal justice issues because the fear of crime is one of the dominant forces shaping much of our contemporary life and working against the practice of hospitality for many people.

No one person can become immersed in every issue which exists. To thoroughly discuss each of the major issues of our time would require a series of books. Looking at those issues and at the persons whose lives are affected by them from the perspective of hospitality does have the potential to transform our society. It's not important that each one of us attempts to tackle every social issue that exists. It is important that we learn how to look at issues from the perspective of hospitality, to recognize the presence of Christ in other people. It's also important that we select one or two specific ways in which we can reach out and be a healing presence in society. In addition to the suggestions made in the discussion of criminal justice issues, consider these possibilities:

- Develop a relationship with one person or with one family in poverty. You may do it through a formal mentoring program of a church or a social service agency, or you may choose to do it on your own with a person or family you encounter.

- Become active in an organization which is working to change the root causes of poverty. Volunteer time, give financial support, and consider being on the board of directors. Bring a perspective of hospitality to the organization.

- Develop a friendship with a person or a family of another ethnic background. Again, it's possible to do this through formal programs in some communities, but it may be most meaningful if you develop such a relationship on your own.

- Become active in an organization which is working to improve race relations. In most communities there is a particularly great need for efforts involving black–white relationships. If no organizations are doing work in this area, consider the possibility of initiating some efforts yourself!

- Develop a friendship with a person who is seriously disabled. Do not look at the relationship as one in which you are going to provide the "help" but rather as one in which each of you will receive blessings. If you are disabled yourself, seek opportunities to help those who are not disabled feel comfortable around you and begin to identify with you as a

person who has a disability rather than being focused
on the disability itself.

- Build a relationship with an elderly person who
  does not have family living nearby. This could be
  a person in your neighborhood or in your church.
  Include that person in your family life, and seize
  the opportunity to learn from that person's life
  experiences.

- Volunteer to work at a women's shelter. Create
  friendship and help women who have been in
  abusive relationships as they seek to build their
  self-confidence and ability to trust others. This
  can be a wonderful opportunity to show hospitality
  to people for whom it can make a difference.

And the list could be continued. Remember, none of us can
do everything. All of us can do something. As a life grounded in
hospitality causes us to recognize the presence of Christ in
others, we should be willing to reach out beyond our normal circle
of acquaintances and friends. There are angels to be found and
blessings to be received!

Some Statistics on Church Growth and Decline

- In a Christian Community study of churches across North America, 85% of the church members surveyed agreed with this statement: "In our congregation, people go out of their way to be friendly to strangers and new-comers." In growing churches, 98% agreed.

- In the same study, people were asked to indicate agreement with the more personal statement: "At church, I take the initiative to talk with those I do not know well." The level of agreement dropped to 68% on this item among all people who participated but only dropped to 92% in growing congregations. In rapidly declining churches, the level of agreement was often below 50%.

- When asked in that study how welcome a person with a drug or alcohol problem would be in the congregation, 90% of those in growing churches said such a person would be warmly welcomed. Only 38% of those in declining churches felt that way.

- 95% of those in growing churches felt that a single parent would find a warm welcome; the figure drops to 62% in churches which are in decline.

- While the size of the church, the programs of the church, the personality of the minister, and many other factors play a role in the interest of people in joining, no single factor is as important as the answer to this question: **Is this a friendly church?** Is this a church which understands and believes in hospitality?

Chapter Eight
Hospitality and the Faith Community

> **Concept:** Hospitality should be at the heart of the faith community and has the power to transform congregational life.

Kristen Leverton Helbert, a friend and colleague of both Fred and Steve, moved with her husband to a new community immediately after they married. Kristen's roots were in the Quaker and the Church of the Brethren traditions; her husband Chad had grown up in a Disciples of Christ congregation. The two of them began searching for a church home in their new community.

A large number of resources, including some Steve and Fred have written, emphasize the importance of churches making a prompt response to visitors and point out that a letter from the pastor, while a nice gesture, isn't a sufficient response. One of the suggestions frequently made is that a volunteer from the church take a gift of baked goods such as cookies or a loaf of bread to the people who visited. It's a simple thing to do and an excellent way to convey interest in the visitors.

Kristen and Chad, however, were not receiving any cookies! Several months and many church visits later, Kristen remarked to Steve that they were still searching for a new church home. They had visited several congregations and were disappointed at the lack of hospitality and the lack of follow-up response in each case. No one had personally welcomed or invited them to participate in other groups or activities of the church. The only follow-up they received came as form letters, and not all churches even did that.

Kristen and Chad are an attractive, successful young adult couple with strong church backgrounds—exactly the kind of new members that most churches claim to be wanting. They are also used to interacting with the public and don't radiate the "don't come near me" signal that some visitors do. Yet the initial welcomes they received and the follow-up on their visits ranged from superficial to nonexistent.

The one exception, an American Baptist congregation, became their church home. The welcome there was genuine and came from several persons, not just the pastor. After their second visit, people from the church came to their home to talk with them. Their denominational backgrounds are not American Baptist, but that doesn't weigh as heavily as the quality of the welcome they received there.

Fred's friend Carl started attending a church in Richmond, Virginia, and initially felt welcome there. He and his family became active and seemed well accepted. When the Gulf War came, Carl found himself disagreeing strongly with the views on the war which were being expressed in worship. Carl was a pacifist and was uncomfortable with what seemed to him a pro-war sentiment that apparently was held by several in the church. He respected the right of people to disagree with him, and he expected people to respect his right to hold other views. He was disappointed.

People in the church, including the pastoral leadership, became quite angry with Carl for his peace position. Carl knew it had gone too far when church members began making threatening phone calls to his home. He was deeply disappointed and left the congregation.

Carl and his family decided that they should seek out a congregation with a tradition as a peace church. They identified Mennonite, Brethren in Christ, and Church of the Brethren as possibilities. The warmest welcome was extended by a Church of the Brethren congregation. Within three weeks, he and his wife had made a decision—they had found a true church home. Not everyone in the church embraced the peace position of the denomination, but there was a healthy openness to differences of opinion and a hospitality that was deep rather than superficial. He later became a pastor in the denomination.

Beverley and Mike had been active in the same congregation for twenty-five years. Their daughter Shelley and her husband Bob had both grown up in that church, had been married in it, and continued to be active members. Their son Jeff moved back to the community after graduation from college. Beverley, Mike, Shelley, and Bob were more than a little shocked when Jeff explained to them that he had come to the conclusion he was gay. He didn't want to make an issue of it, but he also didn't want to hide it. Jeff's brother-in-law Bob was the first to be comfortable with the revelation of Jeff's orientation, but the others in time came to feel the same way. Beverley and Mike couldn't help wondering if they had done something which "caused" Jeff to become homosexual, but they eventually accepted his reassurances that no single factor had caused his orientation. Jeff was convinced that he didn't really decide to become a homosexual but simply recognized that he was a homosexual.

He started a job with a local company and became active in the same church the rest of his family attended. Initially people in the congregation were very enthusiastic about having him back. He was invited to join the choir and also to teach a Sunday school class, both of which were activities he greatly enjoyed.

Then word slowly began to move around the church that Jeff was gay. People began approaching Beverley, Mike, Shelley, and Bob to extend their sympathies to them, as though Jeff had a serious, perhaps incurable illness.

No one said anything directly to Jeff until the Sunday school superintendent had lunch with him. The superintendent explained that a few parents had expressed reservations about Jeff being on the teaching team for the middle school class. There was concern, the superintendent said, that perhaps Jeff would influence children in the class to become gay or that perhaps the children were not quite safe with a person who was a homosexual as their teacher. Jeff did his best to reassure the superintendent that being around a homosexual person was not going to cause someone to become homosexual and that he had no desire to influence the sexual orientation of anyone else. He said that he was offended at the implication that he might do something to harm the children.

The superintendent told Jeff that these concerns were not his own at all and apologized for appearing to be offensive. He also said he felt it best for Jeff not to continue on the teaching team. Jeff agreed, but he was heart–broken. He felt even worse when some of the children approached him, wanting to know why he had quit, and he didn't know what to say to them.

It felt to Beverley and Mike as though the pastor began making more negative references to homosexuality in his sermons than he had before Jeff's sexual orientation had become known. The pastor did not devote an entire sermon to the topic, but he was making his negative views clear. Jeff stopped attending. Beverley, Mike, Shelley, and Bob all became aware that people were acting differently around them than they had in the past. Mike had been the board chairperson elect, but a different person was nominated to be the new board chairperson.

Jeff emphasized to his parents and his sister that he did not want them to stop being involved in the church because of his situation. He thought that he needed to find a congregation in which he could be better accepted. Beverley, Mike, Shelley, and Bob, however, found that they themselves were no longer feeling accepted in the congregation. They did not like the congregation's response to Jeff or to the rest of the family.

All of them found a new home in a United Church of Christ congregation. While that denomination's official position on homosexuality was more accepting than it had been in the denomination they left, the members of the local church they started attending were far from being of one mind on the topic. There were members who did not approve of homosexual behavior and disagreed with the official denominational positions relative to that issue. All of the people in the church, however, immediately extended personal warmth to Beverley, Mike, Shelley, Bob, and Jeff. They were delighted to have them in their congregation. Even those who were not sure how they felt about homosexual behavior as a theoretical issue recognized that Jeff was a wonderful, caring person, and they extended warmth and acceptance to him. The whole family felt affirmed rather than judged.

More Than a Program

The three examples just shared all reflect congregational problems in the practice of hospitality:

- Kristen and Chad had difficulty finding a congregation which would display more than superficial warmth to them. They ended up finding a meaningful church home in a congregation different than the traditions in which they had been raised.

- Carl and his family initially found a welcoming congregation, but the hospitality was only on the surface. When he began to express disagreement on an issue within the life of the church, he encountered not just difference of opinion but outright anger. He could have lived with the difference of opinion, but he could not live with threatening phone calls.

- Jeff's family had a long history with the congregation. Clearly the issue of homosexuality is one on which people of good faith are not always in agreement. Jeff, however, had a kind and gentle spirit. He was not a person to be feared. Tragically the congregation's fear of Jeff's sexual orientation caused them not only to exclude him but in time to make the rest of his family feel excluded as well.

Many factors are involved in the decision of people to choose a church home and to remain active in congregational life. Certainly there are theological or faith differences among denominations which can make a difference. The peace position of the Church of the Brethren was no doubt a better fit for Carl's own belief system than that in the church he had been attending. The views of homosexuality within the United Church of Christ were definitely more open than those in the local congregation which Jeff and his family left. Sometimes such differences can be strong enough that a new church home is the only answer.

Yet differences of opinion on theological issues are not what caused Carl or Jeff to seek a new church home. They sought new church homes because they experienced fear and rejection from people within the congregation. People in the churches to which they moved their membership were not all in agreement with them on the issues. They would have preferred staying where they were if they had felt accepted and loved in spite of the differences of opinion.

We can't readily change the basic theological or faith orientation of our congregations. Such changes, even when desired by many people, take place over long periods of time. What we can change is the willingness of people to extend a level of warmth, of hospitality, that goes beyond the superficial and that can embrace differences in perspective. If people leave our churches, it should be because of genuine faith differences, not because they have experienced rejection or felt themselves the objects of fear.

While congregational studies, policies, and programs can help make hospitality a reality, it is a mistake to see hospitality as simply another program for the faith community. The practice of hospitality, the acceptance and love of others, including strangers, is fundamental to who we are as Christian people. Our society teaches us to be fearful of strangers, but the New Testament teaches a different approach:

> *Do not neglect to show hospitality to strangers, for by doing that some have entertained angels without knowing it.*
>
> Hebrews 13:2

As shared earlier in this book, hospitality to the stranger is assumed throughout the Old and New Testament Scriptures. Again and again, as in the Parable of the Good Samaritan, the questioning is not on the worthiness of the stranger but on the faithfulness of the one encountering the stranger. The Samaritan did not ask of the man who was injured: "Did you bring this on yourself? Why weren't you traveling with someone else for safety?" The Samaritan simply responded to the human need which was encountered. The priest and the Levite who passed by are the ones whose behavior is called into question by our Lord.

Whether we start with the assumption that the unknown person will be an enemy or a friend makes a difference! When anyone comes to our church or shows an interest in religious concerns, our starting assumption certainly should be that such a person shares with us a pull toward the heart of God. Such a person is a potential friend, perhaps sent to us by God for the enrichment of our lives.

The work of hospitality continues long after people have become members or constituents of our congregations. We must continually be sensitive to the presence of Christ in one another, and we must be respectful of the differences of opinion and perspective which inevitably arise in any gathering of people. We should seek to be enriched by those differences rather than driven apart by them.

The Impact of Hospitality

The accounts of Carl and of Jeff rather dramatically show the negative consequences of a lack of true hospitality. There are numerous other situations which are less striking but just as real in negative impact. People like Kristen and Chad experience a lack of warmth in many churches across North America every week. There are also people who find that the churches in which they participate have inner circles which cause them to feel excluded and unwelcome. People can participate in a church for years and still feel not feel part of the congregation's social life.

In the process of studying congregational health, Christian Community (the organization of which Steve Clapp is president) has surveyed active members of churches across the North America. The chart which follows summarizes the amount of agreement with three survey items in churches by category: congregations in decline; the average among all congregations; and congregations which are growing. Over fourteen hundred congregations participated in this study.

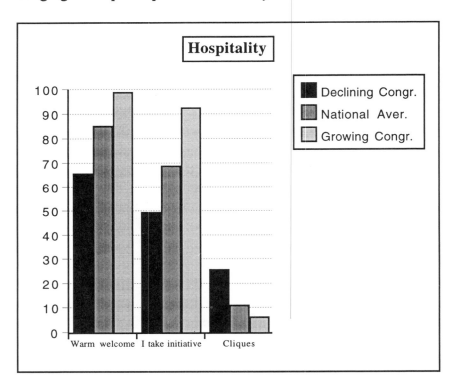

The items:

• *In our congregation, people go out of their way to extend a warm welcome to visitors and newcomers.* Almost 98% of the active members in growing congregations hold that view of their church in contrast to 66% of those in declining congregations.

• *At church, I take the initiative to talk with those I do not know well.* Responses fall some for each category on this item about personal initiative in welcoming others. The percentage is still 92% in growing congregations, but falls to 50% or below in declining congregations.

- *In our congregation, there are cliques or exclusive groups which make one feel unwelcome.* Only 6% of the active members in growing congregations have the perception that there are cliques or exclusive groups. In congregations which are in decline, the figure rises to 26% and is sometimes higher.

The same surveys show that persons who have been a part of a congregation for ten years or more generally indicate that they have seven or more good friends in the congregation. That's part of the closeness which the church at its best should make possible–the enjoyment of participating in the body of Christ. When our own needs are well met by many close friends in the church, however, it's easy to fail to reach out to others. Very few people intentionally exclude others, but the results can be very painful to some members and a complete turn-off to potential members.

Consider what the examples shared in this chapter, the statistical information provided, and some of the larger trends in our society suggest for our faith communities:

1. Churches which are growing have learned how to make the practice of hospitality part of the life of the entire congregation. People feel comfortable taking the initiative in reaching out to others, and visitors immediately feel a welcome that goes beyond the superficial. The life of the congregation is truly open to new people, and members expect that visitors will become friends.

2. People are making their church choices with less and less regard for denominational ties. This does not mean that denominational ties are without importance. Kristen and Chad first searched for a church home within the traditions with which they were most familiar. When they did not find a comfortable church home within those traditions, however, they explored other possibilities. Our churches cannot take for granted that people who grew up within the denomination will stay in the denomination.

Some people feel that we are living in a "postdenominational" time. Certainly it is true that many large Protestant denominations have experienced significant membership decline over the last two decades. That has been true for the Disciples of Christ, the Episcopal Church, the Evangelical Lutheran Church, the Presbyterian Church, the United Church of Christ, the United Methodist Church, and many other denominations.

There has also been considerable growth among many local congregations which call themselves nondenominational. Many of those congregations are relatively new, and they offer considerable energy and vitality. When a church is just starting or is growing rapidly, the hospitality of the congregation is generally very broad. New people are expected and wanted, and that is clearly communicated. People who choose these nondenominational churches are generally not so much rejecting a traditional denomination as feeling attracted to the hospitality and the energy of a newer congregation.

3. It's easy for a local church or even an entire denomination to start looking inward and to become defensive. This is a kind of "circle the wagons" mentality which is almost always self-defeating. We live in a time of extremely rapid social change, and many people are almost desperate for what sociologist Alvin Toffler referred to as "stability zones," places where the pace of change is much slower than in society as a whole. Many people want to see their local congregations as those stability zones. These congregations are often characterized by:

- A reluctance to accept many changes in the style of worship. There is considerable evidence that younger people respond more positively to styles of worship which are more informal and utilize drama and more contemporary music. When people want to see the church as a stability zone, they are often resistive to such changes. The more contemporary efforts are often branded as immature or "dumbing down" or "theologically superficial." What is really going on in the life of the congregation, however, usually has more to do with resistance to change than with anything about theology.

- An initial suspicion toward visitors and newer members. While new people are given a reasonably warm initial greeting in such churches, members are in fact adopting a "wait and see" approach toward them. Will they keep coming? Are they enough like us? Will they bring change?

- An excessive concern about the physical facilities. Outreach programs for children and youth which result in possible damage to the physical facilities are quickly censored in such congregations. Church security systems are often installed to help people feel safer when the church location continues to be in a neighborhood in which relatively few of the church members live.

Rather than being people on a pilgrimage or a journey, such congregations have become a more landed people, who feel a need to protect their turf. The church building, the continuity of the membership, and the predictability of worship and other programs become of greater importance than outreach and mission.

Criticism of such congregations, however, is not a very helpful way to bring about change. People cling to stability zones because they feel threatened, indeed fearful, in other areas of their lives. The way to help people cling less desperately to their stability zones is to help them be less fearful, more confident about the future, and better able to recognize the presence of Christ in others.

4. There is always the danger of fear driving our decision-making in the congregation as well as in our own lives and the broader society. Jeff and his family felt excluded because of the fears of many in the church community about homosexuality. Had they been able to see beyond the issue to recognize the presence of Christ in Jeff, their response would have been a different one.

Fred has suggested to people in seminars that he conducts that many of us are spending too much time deciding what fish we want to catch rather than just putting out the net and taking the fish we reach. Many of us have become too concerned about excluding certain types of people and making value judgments. This applies not only to our attitude toward homosexual people but also to our attitude toward persons who have drug and alcohol problems or who are single parents. The statistical information shared opposite the first page of this chapter notes large differences in attitudes toward people who have problems with addictions and toward single parents between churches which are growing and churches which are in decline. People in churches which are growing are far more likely to feel that people from such backgrounds can find welcome and acceptance.

When we truly learn to recognize the Christ in others, then diversity does not represent a threat to us. Seeing Christ in others enables us to open ourselves to the blessings we can receive from those who are different and enables us to be the channels through which God can share blessings with others.

5. When hospitality is superficial rather than deep, we may gain new members, but we will not successfully integrate them into congregational life. Visitors are often attracted to long established churches because they sense that there are stability zones and relationships that matter. They observe people caring about one another and a large number of social groupings that may be more informal than part of the church's official program. This can be especially true in churches which have many members who are connected by family ties. Visitors want to be part of that kind of community.

In *A Christian View of Hospitality–Expecting Surprises*, Michele Hershberger shares this perspective on what often happens to new people who are attracted to such churches:

> *We are friendly to them and seek to include them as much as we can. But the very thing that attracts them also puts them outside the circle. The very thing that they want so much to be a part of, they can't be a part of completely, no matter how hard*

*they try, because they don't have the same last
names. They don't catch the inside jokes.* [p. 187]

The key to change, of course, is to have a hospitality which
moves beyond the superficial, which enables us to recognize the
presence of Christ in others. That perspective brings enthusiasm
for new people and a willingness to integrate them into the social
life of the congregation as well as the program life.

**6. Our churches, at their best, should be forces for peace
and justice within the broader society.** Politicians and the
news media may promote fear, but the church should not be part
of that process. Those of us who belong to the church should be
alert for opportunities to help people be more at peace with one
another and less driven by fear in the decisions that they make.
We should be concerned about how our government agencies and
social service institutions treat those charged with crimes and
those victimized by crimes. We should be concerned about
juveniles who are in trouble with drugs, the law, or both.

Our congregations should be places where people can talk
about difficult topics that are avoided elsewhere. Our churches
should be places where:

- Problems between blacks and whites and those involving
  other races can be openly and honestly discussed. Our
  churches should be seeking ways to connect people of
  different races, whether they belong to the same church
  or not.

- Young people can feel comfortable talking about sexual
  decision-making, dating, and marriage. If we are truly

concerned about the moral development of youth, then the church should be a moral leader and a safe place for young people to receive the information they need to make intelligent decisions in these important areas.

- Problems in our schools and educational concerns can be discussed. Our churches generally have both parents and educators involved and have the potential to offer a forum not as controlled by political agenda and posturing as happens in the broader community. Juvenile crime and related issues also need to be discussed in our church settings.

Sometimes our congregations decide to become active forces for peace and justice in the community by an institutional presence or involvement. At other times, our congregations may be the settings which equip us individually to be forces for peace and justice in the broader society.

You Can't Reach Everyone, But. . .

"I would ask Betty to visit our church, but I'm just sure she wouldn't want to come. She grew up in a huge church in another denomination, and we're just too different from that." Thus Mary felt it wouldn't be helpful to invite a neighbor to visit her congregation, even though Betty had not participated in any church for many years.

Such logic is sometimes right. Not every church is right for every person. Most of us know people who:

- really want to be part of a large church with many programs from which they can pick and choose.

- greatly prefer being involved in a small church in which it's possible to know the names of almost all members.

- want to have a very formal order of worship with liturgical readings and the minister and choir in robes.

- want to have a very informal order of worship without a bulletin and with casual dress for everyone.

- want to be part of a church which places a great emphasis on individual salvation.

- want to be part of a church which places a great emphasis on peace and justice concerns.

And no congregation can be a match for ALL of the above items. But there is one question asked more than any other by people who visit a congregation:

> **Is this a friendly church?**

If the answer is YES, they may not be as concerned about other characteristics. If the answer is NO, they won't be interested no matter how good a match the church is in other ways.

Mary did end up inviting Betty to join them one Sunday for worship and brunch. She did; she kept returning to the church; and she ended up joining! We shouldn't too readily assume that people will not like our congregation! We need to reach out with warmth to those who do not have a church home–and let them decide whether or not they want to become part of our church family. In our experience, when strangers visit a church, there are some things they want and some they do not want:

1. When visiting a church, most people don't want to be ignored. People expect those who are sitting near them to share brief introductions before or after the service or Sunday school class.

2. When visiting a church, almost no one wants to be overwhelmed. Introduce the new person to a few other people–not to every single person around you.

3. People especially do not want to feel ignored during a designated fellowship time. If they go to a gathering spot for coffee and donuts, they assume that some people will visit with them. They will feel rejected if congregation members are all in tight groups with people they already know.

4. People don't want to feel as though they are being required to pass an acceptance test. Most will feel resentful of conversations which make it appear that someone is attempting to do research on family background and church activity. Churches with a strong ethnic membership sometimes act as though those people who have last names that sound a certain way are more acceptable than others. Communicate a clear affirmation of the visitor.

5. Some people are anxious about how others will respond to certain aspects of their background. A person may be divorced, a single parent who has never married, unemployed, an

alcoholic, or an ex-convict. We do not want in an initial conversation to push someone to fill in the gaps in his or her history. It's better to let the other person share family information as he or she wishes.

6. Parents are always pleased when people show interest in their children.

7. *People almost universally appreciate an invitation to share a meal either that day or at a mutually agreeable date later in the week.*

8. People appreciate being remembered with a phone call the week following their visit. It feels good to know that someone remembered you and took the time to call and reinforce how good it was to have you present. That can be an opportunity to extend an invitation to a meal or a Sunday school class.

9. People appreciate returning the following week and finding that people to whom they were introduced remember them and are delighted to see them again.

10. Visitors may need more assistance from the pastor, greeters, and ushers than regular attenders do. Be respectful of the need for those persons to give priority to the needs of visitors.

Being Proactive

Here are proactive things you can do to help your congregation in its outreach efforts:

1. Pray! Pray for the outreach efforts of your congregation. Pray for people you know who are not involved in any congregation. Pray for God to give you opportunities to reach out to others. Pray for opportunities to show hospitality to people who are very different from yourself.

2. Make a list of people you know who do not belong to any church. You can use this list as a basis for your own outreach and also can share the names with your church.

3. Study books and take training through your church to learn how to more comfortably share your faith and invite others to church. Urge others in your church to study books like this one and our *Widening the Welcome of Your Church*, which focuses on hospitality and congregational life.

4. Invite a person, couple, or family you know who does not have a church home to come to church with you and be your guest for brunch or dinner afterwards.

5. Follow up on the person, couple, or family you invite to keep them involved in your church. If your church really isn't right for them, express your thanks for their having given it a try. One visit, however, usually isn't enough for people to know. Encourage them to come several times, and be sure you introduce them to others in the congregation. Then invite other new people!

6. Let other church leaders know you would like to help with outreach in whatever ways you can. You may be able to help prepare brochures about the church, to make visits to persons who have come to your church, or to do other tasks.

7. Take the initiative to welcome new people who come to your church. Don't wait on them to approach you–go to them.

8. Learn to be less judgmental and to appreciate the differences among people, and encourage others to do the same! If your church grows, it will become more diverse with people of different ages, economic levels, educational backgrounds, ethnic identities, appearances, and interests. Celebrate differences!

9. Be supportive of efforts to change worship and programs to be of greater interest to new people.

10. Help lower the level of fear in society by the way in which you live and by your relationships with others.

Let Us Know

We would like to know what experiences you have in living out a deeper hospitality as an individual and as part of a faith community. If you have an experience you'd like to share, write to us at:

Fred Bernhard and Steve Clapp
LifeQuest
6404 S. Calhoun Street
Fort Wayne, Indiana 46807

DadofTia@aol.com

Study Guide

Suggestions for Using This Study Guide

1. This *Study Guide* is designed for use by individuals and groups wanting to think more deeply about the issues raised in *Hospitality: Life without Fear*. While a few community-based groups may decide to share in this study, most groups will likely be church-based: Sunday school classes, Bible study groups, church boards, membership committees, and mission groups. Some of the activities are clearly more appropriate for use by groups than by individuals.

2. This *Guide* is designed for up to thirteen sessions, but you can choose to do a smaller number. Nine of the sessions relate to specific sections of the book (the *Introduction* plus eight chapters); four (Sessions 5, 8, 12, 13) delve further into issues raised by the book, sometimes with the help of invited resource persons. We recommend that you be sure to do Sessions 1, 3, 4, 6, and 9. Church groups will be want to include Session 11.

3. Remember that every group has both active and passive learners. Try to involve participants in a variety of ways, remaining sensitive to personalities and preferences. Encourage, but do not force, participation. Allow "I pass" as an acceptable response.

4. Having class members use different translations of the Bible will enrich your discussion and give new perspective.

5. The session plans assume that a chalkboard or newsprint is available.

6. While your sessions will be smoothest if group members read the assigned chapters in advance, it's not generally wise to assume that all have done so! Give appropriate summaries to help those who have not read the material and to refresh those who have done so.

7. We recommend that you open and close each session with prayer.

Session One
Introduction to *Hospitality: Life without Fear*, pages 7-15

1. "What do you fear?" Make a list of the things that you fear (on chalkboard or newsprint if doing this as a group). Then go through the list:
   - Mark with an "H" each fear that seems to you healthy.
   - Mark with a "UH" each fear that seems to you unhealthy.
   - Mark with a "?" each fear that could be healthy or unhealthy depending on the circumstances.
   - Mark with a "M" each fear that is a MAJOR one to you.
   - Mark with an "L" each fear that you think is LIKELY to happen.
If doing this as a class or group, invite everyone to contribute to the list of fears.

Then do hand counts to see how many feel that each fear is healthy, unhealthy, . . . Talk about the responses.

2. Share the stories of Steve and Fred from pages 7-8. Invite people to share similar experiences which they have had or which they have heard about from others. What things are more feared today than they were twenty years ago? What things are less feared today than they were twenty years ago?

3. Look at the list of categories which play on our fears (politicians, television dramas and motion pictures, . . .). What personal experiences have you had of fears being caused or reinforced by those sources? What other persons or forces in society play on our fears?

4. Read **Psalm 111**, noting especially verse 10–"The fear of the LORD is the beginning of wisdom; all those who practice it have a good understanding." Many people think the word *fear* in this context means obedience or love or commitment. Why is this kind of fear important? Should a person who is knowingly disobedient fear God? Why, or why not?

5. Look at the definition of *hospitality* provided in the Introduction. In what ways could the practice of that kind of hospitality transform your life? The life of your family? The life of the church? Why is the practice of such hospitality not always safe?

Session Two
Chapter One in *Hospitality: Life without Fear*, pages 16-33

1. Look at the "Safety Tips for Hotel Guests" on page 16. What fears do you experience when you travel? Do you feel safer in your own home or in a hotel room? Why? Do you feel safer flying or driving? Why? What are reasonable precautions to take when traveling?

2. Do the "What Do We Fear?" exercise on pages 22-25. If you are in a group, talk about your responses with others (ideally in groups of three or four people).

3. What factors in our society contribute to loneliness? In what ways do e-mail and the Internet contribute to loneliness? In what ways do e-mail and the Internet help people better connect with others? Note the example on page 29 of the 82-year-old woman not yet adjusted after the death of her husband. How do people best deal with the loneliness or emptiness that comes with the loss of a parent, a spouse, or a child?

4. Reflect on **Hebrews 13:2**–"Do not neglect to show hospitality to strangers, for by doing that some have entertained angels without knowing it." Then look at the definition of hospitality on page 32. Is this definition consistent with the message of Hebrews 13:2? Why, or why not? How does this way of viewing strangers differ from the way of secular society?

5. Do you know anyone who has had an experience like Mable's (as described at the start of the chapter)? If you are in a group, share such experiences with others. What might have prevented that experience for Mable? Is there any way to be completely safe? Why, or why not? What price do we pay when we are too driven by our fears? How does a person build confidence after an experience like Mable's?

Session Three
Chapter Two in *Hospitality: Life without Fear*, pages 34-53

1. Invite people in the group to share any experiences they have had with extreme sports like mountain climbing, sky diving, bungee jumping, or BASE jumping. If people have not had personal experience with such sports, then ask them to share what they know about such sports through other people. Note some of Melanie's observations about the attraction of mountain climbing. What do you think are the reasons for the popularity of extreme sports? How can these activities produce spiritual experiences? Do such activities help people overcome fears? Why, or why not?

2. Note this quote from page 38: "Many of us, however, do not seek to develop the spiritual life with the same energy that we put into gaining an education, earning a living, participating in sports, or even keeping the house clean. Thus the spiritual life becomes one part of who we are, but not the center of our being." How do you feel about that statement? Use tape to put a line on the floor that is numbered from **1** to **10**. Make the line long enough that people can stand along it. Let **1** represent a very low amount of effort, and let **10** represent a very high amount of effort. Ask people to stand along the line to show the amount of effort which they typically expend on:
- Job or career
- Home upkeep and improvement
- Sports (observing or participating)
- Physical fitness
- The spiritual life

Provide opportunity to talk about responses as people stand in place before moving to the next item on the list.

3. Note the biblical verses on the fear of God which are on pages 39-40. With which Scriptures do you most strongly identify? Why? Then read **1 John 4:16-20** which talks about perfect love casting out fear. How do you reconcile what 1 John says with some of the other biblical verses quoted on fear? Is the meaning of fear different in some of these quotations? If so, in what ways?

4. Pages 43-45 talk about the hospitality shown by Abraham and Sarah. How would we change our hospitality toward strangers today if we took those words seriously? Read **Matthew 25:31-46,** which talks about discovering Christ in other people, particularly in the hungry, the naked, the imprisoned. Do we really believe those words in our society? Why, or why not? Reflect on this statement from page 46: "Our relationships with others are transformed when we seriously consider the

reality that we are encountering Christ in the other person. That should affect all of our relationships, every day of our lives."

5. Review the material on handguns and gun violence on pages 48-51. If you are with a group, be sensitive to the fact that there may be strong, differing opinions on these issues. Why are weapons an appropriate spiritual concern? Why have guns become such an important part of society in the United States? What role do television and motion pictures play in the desire of people to own guns? Why does fear have so much to do with gun ownership?

Session Four
Chapter Three in *Hospitality: Life without Fear*, pages 54-71

1. If you are meeting as a group, bring a cat or dog to share in your time together. Reflect on the efforts of Roberto [see page 55] to use pets as a way to build relationships. Why do so many people respond warmly to pets? Is it easier to show hospitality to pets than to people? Why, or why not? Invite people to share stories of ways that pets have positively linked them to other people.

2. Reflect on the section "Bad Things Do Happen, But. . ." which begins on page 59. What are the roots of some of these fears in our society? Who gains because of these fears? How can a person exercise reasonable caution without being overwhelmed by fear?

3. Read **Ephesians 6:10-17**, noting especially verse 12, which is quoted on page 63. What are the "cosmic powers" at work in our world? How do we cope with forces of evil in our time? Why is it important to be alert to feelings of hate as a warning sign for the spiritual life? How can God protect us against the cosmic powers?

4. Reflect on the story of Margaret, who lost her son and her husband. Invite people to share any similar situations of which they are aware. Do you think Margaret actually came to feel that homosexuality was "all right"? Why, or why not? Is it necessary to approve of someone else's lifestyle in order to love that person? Why, or why not? Why are some people in our society so frightened of homosexual persons? How can the church help us with our fears?

5. Look at the examples of transformed lives on pages 69-71. With which of those do you most strongly identify? What similar examples of transformation have you experienced or observed? What gifts do we receive from strangers?

Session Five
Outside Perspective

Have a guest speaker for this session who can share some insights into a category of persons with whom people in our society are often uncomfortable. Possibilities would include:
• A prison chaplain.

- A person who has been in prison who is well integrated into the community now.
- A person from a social service or religious organization who deals with racial tensions and can speak frankly about race relations in your community.
- A person of homosexual orientation who is comfortable talking about the problems faced in your geographical area by people of that orientation.
- Someone from a local PFLAG group, which is made up of family and friends of persons of homosexual orientation.

Provide a copy of *Hospitality: Life without Fear* to the guest speaker in advance of your meeting, so that person can become familiar with what you have been studying. If you are reflecting on this material as an individual rather than as part of a group, consider inviting a person in one of the above categories to have breakfast, lunch, or supper with you.

Session Six
Chapter Four in *Hospitality: Life without Fear*, pages 72-89

1. Think about times in your own life when you have experienced answered prayer or about experiences with prayer that others have shared with you. If you are in a group, share those with one another. When do people most commonly pray? Why do people pray? Are there particular settings or circumstances, other than church, which cause people to be more likely to pray?

2. Reflect on the stories about the cockatiel and about Hillary and Brad. What instances of problems in showing hospitality have you experienced? Do you think Steve and Sara have any regrets about the effort spent helping the cockatiel? Why or why not? Do you think Hillary and Brad have regrets? Why, or why not? Why is it important to help people even when there are risks involved?

3. Look at the guidelines for prayer on pages 80-84. What additional guidelines would you add to this list? Which of the guidelines is most difficult for you to implement in your own life?

4. Read about prayers of rejoicing in **Philippians 4:4-7**. How do prayers of thanksgiving or rejoicing help us? How do prayers for God's guidance and strength help us? Why is it important to pray for God's forgiveness? It has been said that "it is dangerous to ask God for something, because he may give it to you." What does that statement mean to you? Do you agree or disagree with it? Why?

5. Spend time in prayer. If you are part of a group, assign some of the prayers on pages 85-89 to group members to be prayed aloud. OR share your own prayers.

Session Seven
Chapter Five in *Hospitality: Life without Fear*, **pages 90-111**

1. Prepare as many notecards as there are members of your group. On each card, write one of the following:
   - A good family moment or experience.
   - An awkward or painful family moment or experience.
   - A funny family moment or experience.
   - A memorable family moment or experience.
   - An example of forgiveness within a family.
   - A positive family connection between grandparents and grandchildren.

Depending on the size of the group, you may need several copies of some of the items. Put them in a small box or hat, and have each person draw one. Then invite people to share something based on the card drawn. Explain that these do not have to be experiences in your own family–they can be any family experience you've observed or of which you've heard. If people do not want to share, it's fine of course to say "I PASS." If your group is large, you may want to do this sharing in smaller groups of three to five persons.

2. Reflect on the experiences of Carolyn and her daughter Jill and of Keith and his wife Becky. What similar experiences have you had or observed? In what ways does hospitality, seeing other family members as guests and the children of God, relate to these experiences?

3. Consider the material on children which begins on page 93. Which of the implications for parenting seem to you the most important? Thinking about parenting from the perspective of hospitality, what additional perspectives or guidelines would you suggest? The book quotes a psychologist: "The problem for most of us is that we don't do enough to influence the behavior of our children when they are small and then that we try to regain control when they become teenagers." Do you agree with that view? Why, or why not?

4. Consider the material on spouses and significant others which begins on page 101. People in your group who are not married can add much to this discussion by talking about significant relationships they have or about what hospitality means for a person who is single. The book talks about the problem of spouses receiving our leftovers of time, energy, patience, and caring. Why do spouses so often receive the leftovers? What can be done to prevent this? Note that hospitality teaches to cherish rather than control. Why are control issues so difficult in a marriage or in a committed relationship?

5. Study **Isaiah 25:6** on the power of sharing food together and **Luke 14:13-14** on broad invitations to the banquet. What are the implications of these passages for your life? How do these passages relate to the centrality of the dining room table in Steve's home (pages 107-108)? What object or area of your home has or could have a significance similar to that of the dining room table in his childhood home?

Session Eight
Further Reflections on Chapter Five

Option One: Have an intergenerational session. Bring together grandparents, parents, children, and grandchildren. Talk together about some of the concerns raised in pages 104-106 of the book. Identify together ways that closer bonds can be built across the generations–even in our highly mobile society. Share refreshments or a meal together.

Option Two: Build a session around discussion of the bulleted questions on page 110. Invite a person who has opened his or her home to an exchange student, a foster child, or an individual in need to share experiences with the group. Explore together ways the home can be made into a place of deeper hospitality.

Session Nine
Chapter Six in *Hospitality: Life without Fear*, pages 112-143

1. Share with others examples of rudeness you've experienced in restaurants, grocery stores, traffic, work settings, churches, your neighborhood, airports, hospitals, and/or schools. Why has rudeness become so commonplace in our society? How can hospitality make a difference?

2. If you are doing this study as part of a group, invite individuals or smaller groups to focus on a particular section of this chapter:
   • Behind the Wheel
   • In the Neighborhood
   • The Workplace
   • Dealing with Telephone Solicitations
   • E-mail and the Internet
   • Business and Community Contacts
Have each person or smaller group identify what seems most important from the assigned section and also brainstorm any additional ideas for showing greater hospitality in that area of life. Have observations shared with the whole group.

3. Page 140 reminds us that: "Simple resolutions to be 'friendlier' won't result in deep change in our habits or in the attitudes of others." Read again **Hebrews 13:2.** Why is it so important to recognize the presence of angels or of Christ in others? Why is it so difficult for us to do this on a daily basis? How can prayer aid in the deepening of the spiritual life and in the practice of hospitality?

4. Reflect on the bulleted items on pages 141-142 which raise additional strategies or possibilities for sharing hospitality. Which of those would work well in your life? What additional possibilities can you identify?

5. In the discussion of faith-sharing, page 143 asserts: "We do not have to manipulate in order for those opportunities to come; God will bring them to us if we are open to receiving them." Do you agree with that statement? Why, or why

not? Is that statement reassuring, frightening, or both?

Session Ten
Chapter Seven in *Hospitality: Life without Fear*, pages 144-157

1. Reflect on the experiences of Frank McCourt which are shared in the beginning of this chapter. Contrast his experiences with our relative isolation today from persons with extreme physical needs. Do you have a person who is very poor as one of your four or five closest friends? Do you have a person who is very rich as one of your four or five closest friends? Do you have a person of a different ethnic background as one of your four or five closest friends? What do we miss by not having greater diversity in our lives? How does the lack of diversity in our lives contribute to fearfulness in our society?

2. Reflect on the material about crime, perhaps assigning each of these topics to an individual or a smaller group:
   - Juvenile Crime
   - Problems in Jails and Prisons
   - Severe Sentences

Invite each individual or smaller group to share observations about the assigned topic. Why is it so difficult to make changes in our criminal justice system? What is it appropriate to have some fear of crime? How do those fears immobilize us and cause harm? What changes are realistic?

3. Read **Jeremiah 17:9** on evil and the human heart, and look at the quote from Solzhenitsyn on page 152. Why is it more comfortable to think about there being a group of people in society who are clearly evil than to consider the possibility of evil residing in each of our hearts? Page 152 raises this concern: "We have in fact not thought about the persons who commit crimes as being our brothers and sisters in Christ." What difference would that perspective make?

4. Consider the five suggestions on response to crime which are found on pages 153-155. Which of those suggestions do you think are most important? Which are most realistic? What additional suggestions would you make? What personal experiences have you had which relate to these suggestions?

5. Look at the list of things people can do found on pages 156-157. What would you add to this list? What, if anything, should churches be doing in these areas? What would you like to do as an individual?

Session Eleven
Chapter Eight in *Hospitality: Life without Fear*, pages 158-180

1. Reflect on the experiences of Kristen and Chad (searching for a new church home), Carl (concerned about peace issues), and Jeff (who had a homosexual orientation). What kind of welcome would they experience in your congregation? How would you personally relate to them?

2. What kinds of people do you find it easiest to show hospitality? Most difficult? Page 167 says: "We should seek to be enriched by those differences rather than driven apart by them." Why are those words easier to say than to put into practice? What categories of persons from your community are absent from your church? What does **Genesis 18:1-15** suggest about hospitality to all people?

3. Consider the chart on page 168 which makes comparisons between growing and declining congregations. How would people in your church respond to the three items shown on the chart? What improvements are needed in your church?

4. Pages 169-175 include six statements or perspectives. Which are most relevant for your congregation? Why is it crucial for hospitality to be more than just another church program? How can church programs help make hospitality a reality?

5. Reflect on the lists on pages 177-178 of what people want in visiting a church and on pages 178-180 on ways to be proactive. In which of these areas is your church already doing a good job? You personally? In which areas could improvements be made by the church? By you personally?

Session Twelve
A Visitors Perspective

If you are studying this book as part of a church class or group, gain the perspective of visitors and/or recent members. Invite a couple of people who have visited your church in the past year and a couple of people who have recently joined your church to meet with your group. Share with them Chapter Eight in advance of their meeting with your group. Invite them to share what it was like to visit your congregation. What improvements could be made? What did they appreciate about the warmth of their reception? How do new members feel about the way they have been able to become involved in the programs and the social life of the congregation?

Session Thirteen
Overview

Spend a final session thinking about what has been learned during the course of this study. What issues remain unresolved for you? What further study would you like to do in the area of hospitality.

Resources

An asterisk (*) indicates books available from LifeQuest (page 192).

*Bernhard, Fred and Steve Clapp, *Widening the Welcome of Your Church* (LifeQuest), 1996, 1997, 1999, 2000. This is a very practical book which shows how biblical hospitality can revitalize a congregation. It's designed for individual reading or group study and offers strategies which have proven effective across a wide range of denominations and in churches of all sizes.

*Clapp, Steve, *Overcoming Barriers to Church Growth* (The Andrew Center and LifeQuest), 1994. This is a book for people who have difficulty getting the congregation interested in evangelism and outreach. It includes a very helpful section on low self-esteem in individuals, congregations, and denominations as a sometimes overlooked barrier to church growth.

Foster, Richard J., *Prayer–Finding the Heart's True Home* (HarperSanFrancisco), 1992. This is a truly wonderful book about prayer and the ways in which prayer can move us to personal transformation, greater intimacy with God, and more meaningful ministry to others.

Fox, Matthew, *Confessions* (HarperSanFrancisco), 1996. An autobiographical account by a person who has transformed considerable Catholic and Protestant theology emphasizing a broader acceptance of all people and a recognition of God's presence in the natural world.

Glassner, Barry, *The Culture of Fear* (Basic Books), 1999. This is an outstanding book that examines the role of irrational fear in contemporary culture and explores some of the causes of that fear.

*Hershey, S. Joan, *The First Thirty Seconds: A Guide to Hospitality for Greeters and Ushers* (LifeQuest), 2000. This booklet gives practical strategies to help greeters and ushers, who are on the front lines of hospitality, create a warm experience for all who come.

Hershberger, Michele, *A Christian View of Hospitality–Expecting Surprises* (Herald Press), 1999. An excellent overview of hospitality–primarily, but not exclusively, from a congregational point of view.

Kelly, Thomas R., *A Testament of Devotion* (HarperSanFrancisco), 1941, 1942. Kelly was a Quaker educator, missionary, scholar, and speaker who wrote eloquently of a life centered on devotion and obedience to God. His writing has profound implications for the development of the inner life and for the quality of our relationships with others.

McCourt, Frank, *Angela's Ashes* (Scribner), 1996. This book describes extremely harsh living conditions, the practice of kindness in the midst of great poverty, and the inner strength that pulled Frank McCourt through those days.

Mendel, Richard, *Less Hype, More Help–Reducing Juvenile Crime*. The 93-page report is available online at www.aypf.org or can be obtained from the American Youth Policy Forum, 1836 Jefferson Place, NW, Washington, DC 20036 for $5.00 to cover postage and handling (prepaid orders only, please).

Nouwen, Henri J.M., *In the Name of Jesus* (Crossroad), 1989, 1994. This short book on Christian leadership says much about how we can effectively minister to others in the name of Jesus.

Nouwen, Henri J.M., *Reaching Out* (Doubleday), 1975. This is an absolutely wonderful book dealing with the spiritual basis for hospitality.

Rivers, Caryl, *Slick Spins and Fractured Facts* (Columbia University Press), 1996. An intelligent and helpful look at how news media in particular shape our view of the world in sometimes unhealthy ways.

Bruce Rowlison, *Creative Hospitality* (Green Leaf Press, P.O. Box 6880, Alhambra, CA 91802), 1981. Mainly about the church and hospitality but also talks about the home.

Wendy M. Wright, *Sacred Dwelling: A Spirituality of Family Life* (Forest of Peace Publishing, Leavenworth, Kansas) 1994. This is a very helpful book on the development of spirituality in the home.

About LifeQuest

The mission of LifeQuest is to help congregations, families, and individuals grow in spiritual health in ways that positively transform congregational life, nurture personal faith, relate positively to the rapid changes in society, and make a positive difference in the world. We seek to develop strategies and resources that:

- *Help improve congregational health in areas such as evangelism, stewardship, worship, ministerial leadership, and youth work.*
- *Help individuals deal with the practical, ethical, and spiritual issues raised by the Internet and other aspects of electronic culture.*
- *Help individuals and families in the development of healthy spiritual lives, including the relationship of the spiritual life to such areas as hospitality, the arts, physical health, sexuality, the use of money, the impact of rapid societal change, and the personal calling of people to be God's presence to a world in need.*

LifeQuest works cooperatively with Christian Community, which is the research and development organization of which Steve Clapp is president. For information about quantity orders of this publication or about our other resources, contact:

LifeQuest
6404 S. Calhoun Street
Fort Wayne, Indiana 46807
U.S.A.
219-744-6510 (General Inquiries)
419-872-7448 (For Orders)
DadofTia@aol.com
www.churchstuff.com